OCR Computing for GCSE
A451 - Computer Systems and Programming
A Revision Guide

Alan Milosevic, Dorothy Williams

Published by Bagatelle Publications Ltd 2013

Published by Bagatelle Publications Ltd

http://www.bagatelle.com/

First published 2013

Printed in the United Kingdom

Set using LaTeX. Font 10pt Computer Modern.

Contents

Introduction

This revision guide has been written specifically to support work done throughout the course in A451 - Computer Systems and Programming. It is not intended to replace a first class textbook but when used properly will provide an excellent supplement. The revision guide is divided into chapters and sections. Each chapter and section reflect divisions in the original OCR specification for A451. Notes are distributed throughout the guide usually immediately after each section heading. These notes are then followed by a range of questions taken directly from OCR past papers, together with the examiner's mark scheme solutions. In many cases the notes are relatively minimal since the examiner's solutions provide excellent notes.

The overwhelming majority of the questions are taken from OCR past papers. In each of these instances the question number and paper are displayed together with the number of marks awarded for a fully correct answer. Answers to these questions are provided by the OCR mark scheme for the particular paper. Many of these answers are given in bullet point form. You should assume that each bullet point is worth one mark, with the proviso that if the bullet point contains an ellipsis (...), the text following the ellipsis expanding upon or providing an explanation for the first part of the text is also worth one mark.

The student who works his or her way through this book carefully reading the notes and the past paper questions and answers will give themselves an excellent opportunity to consolidate and review the material learned during the course.

Many thanks to the students of d'Overbroecks College, St. Gregory the Great School, Oxford and also to Andy Powell and Menna Hâf for their invaluable help in reading and commenting on this book.

Fundamentals of computer systems

Before you start

This book has been designed to be used as a revision exercise by students working with teachers and those who are working alone. The notes are reasonably extensive and will hopefully help you understand the theory covered in the course. The questions and answers are taken from past papers provided by the examination board and are an integral component of the notes. It is important that you read the questions and answers together with the notes that precede them. The notes on their own are not sufficient. It is the combination of notes, questions and answers that are important. So, please read everything to get the most out of this book.

Definition

The British Computer Society defines a computer as *'a machine that processes data. It takes data in digital form, which is processed automatically before being output in some way'*. With this definition many things are legitimately computers. The PC on your desk, your laptop, mobile phone, washing machine, digital television, digital radio are all computers. All of them take in data, process it in some fashion and provide output of some kind.

We can think of a computer system in terms of **software** and **hardware**. Software are the programs and applications that run on the computer system. An internet browser, a word processor, a graphics package and the operating system itself (Microsoft Windows, Apple's OS X and Linux are three modern operating systems) are all examples of software. Hardware is the physical part of the computer, the bits you can touch. The keyboard, screen, system unit, RAM modules, CPU and mouse are all examples of hardware.

An advertisement for a personal computer is shown overleaf.

What is software? [A451 Specimen Paper 2010 Q1 (1)]

- Programs (which can be run on the computer)

Give one example of software from the advertisement. (1)

- Suitable example, e.g. PS Anti-virus

Importance

It is difficult to over emphasize the importance of computer systems in the modern world. The functioning of modern civilisation depends on the smooth running of hundreds of millions of computer systems. Computers control our water supply, our electricity and our financial institutions. They support our governments, our tax systems, our health service, our mobile phone networks and the internet. Computer systems are crucial to our modern industries of music, film and games. If there is one field of human activity which under-pins everything we do today it is computer science. Without computers we would be thrust back into the nineteenth century.

Reliability

With this incredible reliance on computer systems comes the need for re-liability. When computer systems control how civilisation functions it is imperative that they are reliable. The various system functions on modern aircraft such as the Airbus are controlled almost entirely by computers. Clearly you don't want system failures to occur when you're about to take-off or land. Similarly, our financial institutions depend on the accurate and timely transfer of financial information from bank to bank. You wouldn't want your money to suddenly disappear because a computer system malfunctioned. Reliability is crucial. An integral part of maintaining reliability is conformance to standards; standards of development, use and maintenance of computer systems.

The traffic lights in a town are controlled by a computer system. The town's council is concerned about the reliability of the system. Explain, using examples from the traffic light system, what is meant by reliability and why the town needs the system to be reliable. The quality of written communication will be assessed in your answer to this question. [A451 Specimen Paper 2012 Q6 (6)]

The examiners expected that the following points would be included:

- Reliability
    - Reliability implies consistent performance
    - E.g. the hardware should perform well under all weather conditions
    - The system should be robust, i.e, the system should not crash easily or often
- Importance of reliability
    - If the system is unreliable, traffic in the town will be affected
    - Unreliable systems are a potential danger and may cause accidents
    - There may be knock on effects, e.g. loss of income for people in the town if people stayed away and the council could become unpopular

Standards

Standards are an agreed way of doing things. In the case of computer systems for example, there are agreed ways of sending and receiving data, called protocols which you should be familiar with from the course. Computer programs running on aircraft, controlling financial transactions and managing robots in factories are very sophisticated and cannot be written by one person. There are protocols for writing software so that many people can work together, each writing part of the program in such a way that the program can be properly tested and can be seen to work. Similarly, there are agreed ways of maintaing computers and of connecting computer devices together. For example, you would expect your USB flash drive to work in any computer system and if your graphics card failed, you would expect the new one you bought from the local shop to physically fit into your computer and work without too much difficulty on your part.

Ethics, Environmental and Legal considerations

In the light of the use of computers everywhere in modern society, a number of ethical, environmental and legal issues need to be considered.

In the Workplace

There are widespread concerns that the increasing use of computers is dehumanising the workplace leading to job losses and the de-skilling of many of the jobs that remain. Additionally, a number of health issues have arisen as people spend more and more time at the computer. These range from Repetitive Strain Injury (RSI) where the repeated use of the mouse and keyboard lead to joint and tendon problems, to back problems due to bad posture. Perhaps more worryingly people often experience a sense of loss of self respect and purpose when computers appear to control the conditions under which they work. Unless addressed this can often lead to depression.

Computer Crime

Computer crime has become a major concern not only for businesses and organisations but also for governments. The reliance of so much of our society on computer technology has given criminals great opportunities for fraud and theft. In recent months some governments have made use of their computer scientists to attack the computing infrastructure of other governments. Wars in the future will be played out as much in Cyberspace as on the battlefield.

Privacy and Anonymity

Privacy is an increasingly contentious issue in modern society. Modern governments have large electronic databases of information on their citizens. This information includes tax and social security records, names, addresses, health records and much besides. There is great concern as to who should be allowed access to this information. With the integration of many once discrete databases into larger all inclusive databases it is now much easier to gather highly sensitive information about individuals quickly and efficiently. How should an individual's privacy be protected?

Intellectual Property

Intellectual property in the digital domain is something few people had spent much time thinking about until the growth of the Internet and peer-to-peer networking allowed people to post and other people to download music, games, films and software. For creative people who have written songs, made films or produced software it is extremely discouraging to find your hard work and effort given away by anonymous strangers. In most western countries there are laws, unfortunately often ineffective, which attempt to protect programmers and musicians from having their work 'stolen' in this fashion, but amongst young people all over the world, downloading of all forms of electronic works is now generally socially acceptable.

Globalisation

The Internet has brought everyone closer together. It is astonishingly easy to communicate with people all over the world and for virtually no cost. Software such as Skype and Facebook allow friends living in different continents to talk to each other, exchange photographs and music and spend time together almost as if they lived next door. Cultures that were once distinct are now meeting each other on a daily basis. This requires each person to be more aware of their behaviour and how it might affect others from different communities.

Environment

Computers have a major impact on our environment. Many of the components in modern computer systems make use of rare earth metals which are in limited supply. The digging out of these metals causes enormous problems of pollution and degradation of the environment. The Internet has thousands of millions of devices communicating on a daily basis. These are powered by electricity which in the main is supplied by the burning of fossil fuels which in turn contributes to climate change. Computer systems are replaced on average every three to five years. Many computer components are now recycled, but significant numbers of computer systems are still dumped each year into landfill sites throughout the world.

A school uses a computer system to monitor the attendance, punctuality and homework of its pupils. Explain how the school might address any legal issues when creating a system which stores personal data about pupils. The quality of written communication will be assessed in your answer to this question. [A451 Jan 2012 Q7 (6)]

As with all questions of this type, there is no set answer and the examiners accepted answers about any relevant areas of legislation (e.g. data protection, freedom of information, child protection, copyright and licensing etc.). As an example of how this question might be answered, they suggested the following points.

- The school should take reasonable steps to ensure that only authorised people can access pupils' personal data
- . . . and should ensure that the school network is safe from hackers, e.g. strong passwords and firewalls
- . . . and should expressly seek permission from the pupil to pass data to third parties, (e.g. when providing references)
- Any images in which students can be identified cannot be used without students' and/or parents' permission
- . . . to comply with child protection legislation

Mary's computer has an 800MHz CPU and 1GB of RAM. She has decided that she wants to upgrade. A computer shop tells Mary that she would be better off buying a new computer, than upgrading the computer that she already has. However, Mary wants to consider the environmental impact as well as the cost.

Discuss the advantages and disadvantages of buying a new computer instead of upgrading and advise Mary on what she should do. You should focus on the environmental impact and the cost. [A451 Specimen Paper 2010 Q2 (6)]

In questions such as these, the quality of your written communication is also assessed. You should consider the question and plan your answer carefully before starting to write. In this particular question, the examiner was looking for the following points.

- **Cost:** If Mary upgrades, she only has to replace a few components. However, this can cost more in the long run, because she will probably need to upgrade again fairly soon. Also, components compatible with outdated hardware e.g. older motherboards, may actually be more expensive. Technology tends to get cheaper. Buying a new computer may allow Mary to sell the older computer or have a second computer for another purpose.

- **Environmental impact:** Buying a new computer could be considered to be wasteful whereas upgrading encourages reuse. However upgrading means unwanted components will be wasted and will need to be disposed of whereas a new computer can allow the old computer to still be used for a different purpose. New computers are generally built to higher environmental standards, although they are usually more powerful and consume more power.

Computing hardware

2.1 THE CENTRAL PROCESSING UNIT

The Central Processing Unit (CPU) is a microprocessor, i.e. an electronic machine made of silicon. The newest microprocessors are made up of many hundreds of millions of transistors packed into a package not much more than a few square millimetres. Very complex fabrication techniques are used to produce something so small.

Its function

The job of the CPU is to get an instruction from memory (FETCH), work out what it means (DECODE) and then do it (EXECUTE). The FETCH-DECODE-EXECUTE (FDE) cycle is repeated over and over and over again. This is all the CPU does. It is a machine, albeit a very complex machine that is designed simply to FETCH, to DECODE and then EXECUTE an instruction. From the moment the computer is switched on until it is switched off, the CPU simply runs the FDE cycle.

The amazing power of a computer system does not come from powerful instructions, but simply from the fact that the CPU can fetch, decode and execute thousands of millions of relatively simple instructions per second.

Characteristics

Microprocessors are characterised by a number of factors of which perhaps the most important are its clock speed, i.e. how many times per second does its clock tick, how many bits the processor can move each clock cycle, how many cores it has and how large its cache is.

Clock speed

Whilst the brain of any computer system is the CPU, its heart is a clock. In our bodies our heart beats roughly once every second. Each time it beats, blood is pumped around the body and we can feel this as a pulse in our wrists and neck. In a similar way, the clock in a computer system 'beats' but much, much faster. The clock inside your computer is probably ticking along quite nicely at roughly 3,000,000,000 (three thousand million) times per second. Each time it ticks, data can move around the system just like blood flows through our veins and arteries. In the case of a computer system the veins and arteries are represented by the data and address busses. When the clock ticks, data flows into and out of the CPU and to and from RAM.

Each computer system runs at a specific clock speed. 3 GHz seems to be fairly common now. 1 Hz is a quick way of saying **'once per second'**, 1 KHz is short for 1,000 times per second, 1 MHz for 1,000,000 (i.e. one million) times per second and 1 GHz for 1,000,000,000 (i.e. one thousand million) times per second. A system that is 'clocked' at 3 GHz has a clock that is ticking 3 thousand million times per second.

Bits

Microprocessors process data and can be characterised as 8-bit, 16-bit, 32-bit or 64-bit. In simple terms, a 16-bit processor means that the processor can process, i.e. calculate with or move around, 16 bits each clock cycle. The newer processors are 64-bit and so 64 bits of data can be processed and moved to and from the microprocessor and RAM each time the clock ticks.

Cores

Most computer systems on sale these days have at least two cores inside them. Each of these cores can be thought of as individual microprocessors. It means that with the appropriate operating system such as Mac OSX, Windows 8 or Linux, each core can run independently from the other for much of the time. More recent computer systems have quad core (i.e. four cores) microprocessors and at the time of writing 8 and 16 core CPUs are available.

Cache

Cache RAM is very fast RAM (see page 21) inside the CPU. Instructions are brought from RAM to the CPU to be decoded and executed. RAM is slower than the CPU which means that the CPU has to wait until the RAM is ready. Bringing chunks of code inside the CPU means that instructions in the chunk can be processed at the full speed of the CPU. Fetching a large number of instructions is slow but this is more than offset by the increased speed of processing. A large cache is more efficient than a small cache, but is more expensive.

Jo buys a notebook computer which has a 3MHz quad-core central processing unit (CPU)

State the purpose of the CPU. [A451 Jan 2011 Q1 (1)]

- To carry out the processing on the computer
- To (fetch and) execute instructions

Mary's computer has an 800MHz CPU and 1GB of RAM. Describe the purpose of the CPU. [A451 Specimen Paper 2010 Q2 (2)]

- Controls the operations of the computer
- Fetches and
- ...executes instructions (to allow software to run)

Mary wants to upgrade this computer so that she can play the latest games. Explain two ways by which the computer can be upgraded to improve its performance. (4)

- Higher processor speed
- ...to increase the number of instructions the processor can carry out in a given time
- CPU with more cores

- ...which share the load of running the game
- More RAM
- ...to increase the number of programs/amount of data that the computer can handle at the same time

The table below contains statements about the functions of the CPU. Tick one box in each row to show whether the statement is true or false. [A451 Specimen Paper 2012 Q7 (4)]

	TRUE	FALSE
It performs arithmetic operations on data		
It fetches and executes instructions		
Input and output devices are plugged into it		
It moves data to and from memory locations		

Answer:

	TRUE	FALSE
It performs arithmetic operations on data	✓	
It fetches and executes instructions	✓	
Input and output devices are plugged into it		✓
It moves data to and from memory locations	✓	

Computer performance

Computers with more cores running at a higher clock speed with larger caches, more RAM and able to process more bits at a time are faster than computers with lower characteristics. More cores means the simultaneous execution of multiple processes. Higher clock speeds mean that more instructions can be processed per core per second. Larger caches mean that more instructions can be run at the full speed of the CPU. More RAM means more that programs can be held in memory simultaneously. More bits means that more data can be processed on each clock cycle.

Describe what is meant by a 3MHz CPU. [A451 Jan 2011 Q1 (2)]

- 3MHz is the clock speed, i.e. how fast the processor is
- It indicates how many instructions may be processed in each second
- It indicates how many clock cycles there are per second

Describe what is meant by a quad-core CPU. (2)

- The computer has 4 cores
- ...which are independent processors within the CPU
- ...working simultaneously, they can perform multiple tasks

Some CPUs have cache memory. Describe what is meant by cache memory. [A451 Specimen Paper 2012 Q7 (2)]

- Cache memory is a small block of very high speed memory
- ...acting as a buffer
- ...between the CPU and the main memory
- It stores data and instructions which are used frequently by the CPU

Explain why cache memory is needed. (2)

- So that the CPU does not have to access the main memory
- ...which is slower than the cache

2.2 BINARY LOGIC

All computer devices run on electricity. Electricity is either on or off. This suggests using a binary system with two symbols where 1 represents on (typically 5 volts) and 0 represents off (0 volts).

Why Binary?

A dictionary definition of binary might give you the following definition.

- **Characterized by or consisting of two parts or components; twofold.**
- **Of or relating to a system of numeration having 2 as its base.**

When we're trying to understand how electronic devices work we need to think in binary. Simply think on or off, true or false or 1 or 0. Thinking this way leads us on to truth tables and logic diagrams.

Truth tables

Truth tables are logical constructions which have inputs and outputs. An input is either True or False as are the outputs. It is a commonly agreed convention that we should represent True by 1 and False by 0.

NOT Truth Table

A NOT truth table takes a single input (which is either True or False) and has a single output (again either True or False). NOT negates (or inverts) its input so we get the following truth table.

Table 2.1: NOT truth table

Input	Output
0	1
1	0

This table simply says that if the input is 0 (i.e. False) the output will be 1 (i.e. True). Conversely if the input is 1 (i.e. True), the output will be 0 (i.e. False).

Computer scientists use truth tables extensively. Microprocessors are made up of many millions of tiny **transistors** that in turn are grouped together in logical blocks called **gates**. To design microprocessors we need symbols to represent gates and the logic gate for NOT is

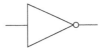

There are two more truth tables that you need to know about, OR, AND but I've also included XOR for the sake of completeness. You will be required to interpret and use NOT, AND and OR gates, but you will not be expected to interpret or use XOR gates in the examination. Each of the truth tables for AND, OR and XOR take two inputs and produce a single output.

OR Truth Table

The OR gate has the following truth table.

Table 2.2: OR truth table

Input		Output
0	0	0
0	1	1
1	0	1
1	1	1

The symbol for an OR gate is

As you can see from the truth table the output of an OR gate is True if **either** or **both** of its inputs are True. Only in the case where both inputs are False is the output False.

AND Truth Table

The AND truth table is shown below. Like the OR truth table it takes two inputs and produces a single output.

Table 2.3: AND truth table

Input		Output
0	0	0
0	1	0
1	0	0
1	1	1

The symbol for an AND gate is

An AND gate produces a True output if and only if **both** of its inputs are True, otherwise the output is False.

XOR Truth Table

Finally we have the XOR truth table. As with the OR and AND truth tables it takes two inputs and produces a single output.

Table 2.4: XOR truth table

Input	Output
0 0	0
0 1	1
1 0	1
1 1	0

The symbol for an XOR gate is

For an XOR gate the output is True if and only if the outputs are **different**, otherwise the output is False.

Logic Diagrams

Take a look at the following logic diagram.

A and B represent single bit inputs to the diagram. C is the single bit output. A feeds a NOT gate and the output of this gate together with the input at B represent the inputs to the subsequent AND gate. The question is, given the possible input values, what are the output values?

The easiest way to do this is to construct a truth table. Since whatever comes in at A is inverted, it makes sense to create a table like the following.

Table 2.5: Problem truth table

Inputs			Output
A	not A	B	C
0	1	0	0
0	1	1	1
1	0	0	0
1	0	1	0

This table tells us that the output at C is 1 (i.e. True) only when A=0 and B=1. This is clearly correct since the output from an AND gate is only 1 (i.e. True) when **both** inputs are 1 (i.e. True). Since A is inverted (also called negated) by the NOT gate, A needs to be 0 so that its inverted value is a 1.

What do you think the following logic diagram does?

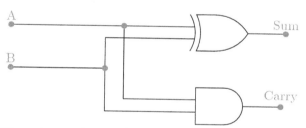

The value at A provides an input to **both** the XOR gate and the AND gate as does the value at B. Let's draw a truth table, this time with four columns, one each for A and B and one each for Sum and Carry.

Table 2.6: Half Adder truth table

Inputs		Outputs	
A	B	Carry	Sum
0	0	0	0
0	1	0	1
1	0	0	1
1	1	1	0

This table tells us that when the input values are 00 we get 00, when they're

01 the output is 01, when they're 10 the output is still 01 and when the inputs are 11 we get 10. Can you see what these gates are doing ?

This small group of two gates is actually working as a simple adding machine. It can only add two binary digits together, but it does do it correctly. This circuit is called a **half adder**. If we wanted to be completely accurate we should add another input representing a possible carry from a previous calculation. Such a circuit would add the carry to the result of the this calculation, i.e. it would use a second half adder circuit to do the calculation. The final circuit is what we call a full adder.

If we were to put eight full adders together the result would be a circuit that added two sets of eight bits (i.e. one byte) together. Modern 64-bit microprocessors can easily add two sixty four bit numbers together which suggests that somewhere in the microprocessor is a circuit with 64 full adders. Each of the OR, AND and NOT gates are made out of transistors. Electronic engineers spend at least part of their time looking at truth tables and logic circuits. It's a very intellectually demanding job, but it is out of such circuits that a microprocessor is made.

The full adder circuit is shown below, purely for illustrative purposes. You **do not** need to reproduce this in the exam. The exam circuits are very simple and straightforward.

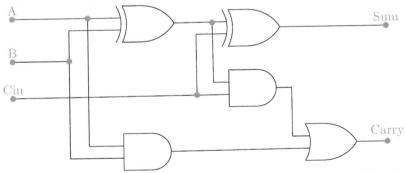

As an exercise you might like to build the truth table for the full adder.

Simple logic diagrams

The examiners will expect you to be able to create simple circuit diagrams from a given circuit and to write down the circuit that corresponds to a given circuit diagram. These will not be complicated and will consist of at most two or three logic gates. The following question is one example of the type of question that you might be asked.

Draw the circuit diagram which will represent the circuit P = NOT (A AND B) [A451 Jun 2011 Q4 (2)]

Here we're being asked to AND two inputs (A, B) together and then negate their output giving us the circuit diagram.

Answer

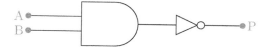

The examiners gave marks for ...

- A B input into an AND gate
- Result from AND gate put through a NOT gate to give P

The full 2 marks were also given for a single NAND gate.

Draw the logic circuit for P = (A OR B) AND C [A451 Specimen Paper 2010 Q10 (2)]

Here we're being asked to OR two inputs (A, B) and AND the output with a third input C. The resulting circuit diagram is the following.

Answer

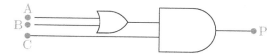

The examiners gave marks for ...

- A and B put through an OR gate in the circuit
- ... and the output put through an AND gate with C

You might be asked to produce a truth table from a given logic circuit as in the following question.

The following logic circuit can be written as **P = (NOT A) AND B.**

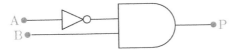

Complete the following truth table for the circuit given above.
[A451 Jun 2011 Q4 (3)]

A	B	P
0	0	
0	1	
1	0	
1	1	

You should notice that since P is the output from an AND gate, P can only ever be 1 if both its inputs are 1. You should also notice that A is inverted before it becomes the input to the AND gate which means that only when A = 0 and B = 1 will P be a 1. With the three other possible combinations of input, P will be always be 0.

Answer

A	B	P
0	0	0
0	1	1
1	0	0
1	1	0

The examiner may also ask you to state the output with a given set of inputs as in the following question.

The following logic circuit can be written as **P = NOT (A AND B)**

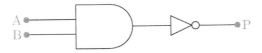

State the output(P) of the circuit if the inputs are:

A=1 B=0 [A451 Specimen Paper 2010 Q10 (1)]

The output from an AND gate is only 1 if both inputs are 1 and since B=0 the output from the AND gate must be 0. However, this is then inverted which means that the value at P will be 1.

A=1 B=1 (1)

Following the same logic, since both inputs to the AND gate are 1, the output of the AND gate must also be 1. But this is then inverted which means that the value at P must be 0.

2.3 MEMORY

RAM and ROM

All the instructions that make up a running application must be held in memory. But when the computer is first switched on, its main memory, **Random Access Memory** or **RAM** will be either empty or indeterminate, i.e. full of random ones and zeros. This is because RAM needs to be continually refreshed and loses its contents when the power is switched off.

There is however another type of memory on the motherboard that is packed full of instructions which the CPU can read. This memory is called **Read Only Memory** or **ROM** for short. When the manufacturer made the computer it will have placed a chip burned full of start up instructions on the motherboard. The instructions in this chip provide a series of tests which the CPU runs before doing anything else. Subsequent instructions check that there is a keyboard attached, that there is a hard disk or appropriate substitute available, whether or not there is a DVD player attached and so on. Essentially these instructions check that we have a working system.

When IBM introduced the first personal computer on August 12 1981, its software engineers had designed matters so that the CPU was hardwired to fetch its very first instruction from address FFFF0 in RAM. All CPUs in modern personal computers follow the same path and when switched on automatically fetch their first instruction from this same address.

Once testing has been successfully completed, the final instructions in the ROM instructs the computer to read into RAM the 512 bytes of instructions found on the first sector on the first track on the first head of any boot device it has found. Usually this means the hard disk. These instructions cause the CPU to read further sectors off the hard disk into RAM and slowly but surely, the RAM starts to fill up with instructions. These instructions are the operating system of the computer. When enough have been read and executed you'll see the usual prompt screen.

A desk-top computer's memory includes ROM and RAM. Tick one box in each row to show whether each of the statements is true for ROM or RAM. [A 451 Jan 2011 Q4 (3)]

	ROM	RAM
Programs and data which are currently in use are loaded here		
All the contents are lost when the power is turned off		
It is used to boot up the computer when it is switched on		

Answer:

	ROM	RAM
Programs and data which are currently in use are loaded here		✓
All the contents are lost when the power is turned off		✓
It is used to boot up the computer when it is switched on	✓	

Why ROM?

Without ROM with its fixed set of instructions the CPU wouldn't know what to do when the power came on. These days, the ROM chip can be reconfigured. However, in the early days of computing these chips could not be altered once configured, hence the name Read Only Memory. They could be read from but not written to. That is no longer the case for the ROM chip on your motherboard, but there are innumerable examples of ROM chips with fixed programs in use in washing machines, toasters, microwave ovens, cars, aeroplanes and so on. Anywhere there is a need for a fixed set of instructions for a CPU to read, you'll find ROM chips.

To summarise, ROM chips are read only, they do not lose their contents when the power disappears (i.e. they are non-volatile) and they provide a fixed set of instructions for CPUs to read when power is first applied. These instructions make up what is commonly called the BIOS (Basic Input Output System).

Why RAM?

ROM gets us up and running, but CPUs always get their instructions from memory, either from RAM or ROM. A small amount of ROM is fine, but we need memory to store all of our running programs, we need memory to store the operating system and to store the document we're working on while we're working.

You may wonder why we can't simply get our instructions off the hard disk. I've said earlier that we take the operating system off the hard disk and load it into RAM. Why not simply forget the RAM and read the instructions directly off the hard disk? The answer is that we could, but hard disks are many thousands of times slower than RAM. If we had no RAM and the CPU fetched its instructions directly off the hard disk our computer systems would effectively grind to a halt and we'd get no work done. By fetching the instructions into RAM first and then reading them from RAM the CPU can run pretty close to its designated clock speed.

To summarise, RAM is used to store the operating system and our application programs. It is also volatile, meaning that when the power is removed each bit of the RAM becomes random and our instructions and data are lost.

Mina's computer has 4GB of RAM. Describe the purpose of RAM in the computer. [A451 Jan 2012 Q8 (2)]

- Stores parts of the operating system currently used by the computer
- Stores programs that are currently running
- Stores data that are currently used by the computer

RAM and computer performance

If we only have a small amount of RAM, we may not have enough for the operating system. If that's the case the computer system is going to have to use the hard disk as its source of instructions and the computer would run incredibly slowly. If we have enough for the operating system but not much more, then we're going to have difficulty running any applications, all of which need to be copied into RAM before they can run. Some applications are very large and need lots of RAM, so again we'll have great difficulty running these types of applications.

More RAM means more applications can be held in memory simultaneously. This is a very good thing because modern operating systems are multi-tasking. We'll have a more detailed look at what multi-tasking is in the section on multi-tasking on page 44 but in simple terms, a computer system that is multi-tasking means that many applications can run apparently simultaneously.

Mina's computer has 4GB of RAM. Mina upgrades the computer to 6GB of RAM. Explain how this upgrade will affect the performance of the computer. [A451 Jan 2012 Q8 (2)]

- The computer will be able to multitask more programs
- ...as there is more memory for programs/data to be loaded into
- Programs will run faster
- ...due to less use of virtual memory

Virtual memory

Multi-tasking needs lots of RAM because the typical user today has their internet browser running at the same time as they are collecting email, listening to music and possibly playing a 3D graphics game. Each application takes up memory so the more memory you have, the more applications you can have running apparently at the same time. What happens if you don't have enough memory?

This is where virtual memory comes into play. Modern operating systems are very sophisticated programs. If such an operating system finds that you want to load the latest and greatest computer game into RAM that's pretty much full running internet browsers and your music programs, it will relocate programs you've not used recently to the hard disk and will replace them by the game program. This will take time, since compared to RAM, hard disks are extremely slow, but once the transfer has been completed you're off and running again. Essentially the operating system uses the hard disk as extra RAM. We call this usage of the hard disk as RAM **virtual memory**. There are various ways in which the operating system can do this, but essentially if your free RAM is running low, the operating system will use the hard disk as extra memory.

Some operating systems have highly efficient ways of using the hard disk as extra RAM and under normal operating conditions will use the hard disk for storing parts of applications that maybe haven't been used in a while. That aside, it's normally advisable to try to make sure that you have as much RAM as you can afford in your system so that you avoid the use of the hard disk as virtual memory since there is always a speed penalty.

Mina's computer has 4GB of RAM. The computer also uses virtual memory. Explain what is meant by virtual memory. [A451 Jan 2012 Q7 (2)]

- A section of the hard disk is used
- ... to store items in RAM which are not currently being used

State why virtual memory is needed. (1)

- Used to allow more programs and/or data to be loaded when the RAM is insufficient

Cache memory

Computer scientists are always looking to try to improve the performance of CPUs and systems generally. Much as hard disks are very much slower than memory, on modern computer systems the CPUs run at typically 2 GHz to 3 GHz. RAM is fast, but it's not that fast, with the result that the CPU has to wait for a few clock cycles before reading or writing to RAM. In order to try to keep the CPU running flat out, computer scientists have put small amounts of RAM, typically a few megabytes, onto the CPU itself. Reading and writing to this RAM called **cache RAM** happens at the full speed of the CPU.

In order to take advantage of the cache RAM, instructions need to be copied out of RAM and placed in the cache. Once there, the CPU will fetch its instructions from the cache. If an instruction isn't in the cache, another group of instructions are pulled from main RAM and replace the instructions in the cache. The CPU then continues to take instructions from the cache. But if we've got to copy the instructions from RAM and put them into the cache is that really any faster than simply reading them one by one from RAM?

The answer is that it all depends on the efficiency of the algorithms that control the cache and the size of the cache. The CPU has some very powerful instructions that can copy large numbers of instructions very quickly into the cache. If the cache is small, a few thousand bytes for example, there isn't a great deal of benefit, because we'll quickly run through the instructions in the cache and have to go back to RAM to copy in more. However, if the cache is relatively large, say ten megabytes, there is a significant benefit. Most programs spend much of their time looping around counting things. Reading these instructions over and over again from cache gives a significant performance benefit over fetching them one by one from the RAM, even bearing in mind that we have to copy them from RAM in the first instance.

Flash memory

Flash memory is a non-volatile (i.e. it doesn't lose its contents when the power is turned off) form of memory that can be electrically erased and re-programmed. The BIOS (page 22) on most modern motherboards is of this type and can be updated by 'flashing' using a specially written program. The USB sticks used by many students to take homework to and from school is also of this type. The memory in such devices can typically be erased and re-written many tens of thousands of times without error.

New memory technologies

New memory devices based on innovative technologies are coming to the market almost every day. The days when computer programs were written on punched cards where the holes in the cards represented ones and the lack of a hole, a zero, are now long gone. Today we have a long list of different devices using a variety of different technologies.

On the motherboard we have Dynamic RAM (DRAM) used in the majority of personal computers which stores data in capacitors in an integrated circuit and needs constant refreshing for the contents to retain their integrity. Static RAM (SRAM) uses a technology called **bi-stable latching circuitry** which doesn't need refreshing to maintain its contents, so long as the power isn't lost. We have DDR SDRAM which stands for Dual Data Rate Synchronous Dynamic RAM much used on graphics cards these days. For not a great deal of money you can buy DDR3, DDR4 versions which give very high performance. New technologies include 1T RAM which although still needing refreshing doesn't use capacitors and RLDRAM which is essentially a high performance DDR RAM.

For long term storage we have flash memory of various flavours used in the BIOS and on removable media such as USB sticks. We also make use of optical memory such as CDs and DVDs which store data in the form of minute pits on a special material. Lasers are used to read and in the case of DVD-RW, write to these disks. Optical storage and retrieval is fairly slow. For faster access we use magnetic storage technologies in the form of hard disks where data is stored as magnetisation patterns of the surface of the disks. Modern hard disks have multiple read-write heads on multiple disks and rotate at typically 10,000 revolutions per minute.

Modern memory technologies mean that you can carry around in your pocket astonishing amounts of information. Digitisation of museums, of image galleries, of libraries is proceeding apace. We can now create and store virtually limitless amounts of digitised data. Such data might represent images, sound, text, video or more even more remarkably, 3D objects, all of which are available to us at the press of a few buttons.

2.4   INPUT AND OUTPUT DEVICES

Every computer system needs some way of getting data into the system and then getting it out again. Personal computers typically have a keyboard and mouse to put data in and screens and printers to get data out. Other common input devices include cameras, scanners and microphones while output devices include screens, speakers, printers and plotters.

Keyboard

The keyboard is still found pretty much everywhere. Personal computers usually have quite a large keyboard of typically 102 keys which includes all of the standard alphabetical characters, numbers (often duplicated on a slightly separate numeric keypad), punctuation keys, movement (arrow keys, home and end) and function keys. The layout of the keys differs from country to country, the standard UK keyboard is based on the typewriter QWERTY design where the placement of the keys were chosen to avoid jamming up the typewriter. In spite of the clear advantages of better more ergonomically designed keyboards, QWERTY retains a dominant share of the marketplace.

Smartphones often have **soft** keyboards, i.e. keyboards which are simply touch sensitive areas of the display screen and are invoked when the user needs to type something. Brought to prominence by the iPhone and its heirs, it is now a common way of interacting with a smartphone. Older phones had a simpler system where the user repeatedly pressed a key on the numeric keypad to select one of the letters which were normally inscribed above. Although slow, such phones benefited from the introduction of predictive text where software on the phone would attempt to predict the word the user was attempting to spell out based on the keys pressed so far.

There are numerous other types of keyboards used in a multitude of different applications. GPS (Global Positioning System) navigation systems used extensively in modern cars, have a small number of buttons which are used to select destination, route options and various system features. Information kiosks often use enclosed dedicated keypads to select from a list of menu items as do the banking system's automated teller machines (ATM).

Mouse

The mouse appeared for the first time in a computing system sold by the German company Telefunken in 1970. It re-appeared in a computer system sold by Xerox Inc. in 1981 along with a host of other technologies that we now take for granted, including a graphics system, networking and a graphical user interface which used windows, icons, menus and pointers for the very first time. Subsequently adopted by Apple Inc., the mouse has become ubiquitous and along with the keyboard, is pretty much the universal choice of input device.

There are various flavours of mouse available. The early mice used a roller ball pressing on small runners which fed information back to the operating system which could then work out where the mouse pointer should be placed on the screen. These have pretty much disappeared now, to be replaced by optical mice which use light emitting diodes and photodetectors to detect movement along the underlying surface.

Other variants on the mouse include tracker balls (essentially an upside down mouse) and gyroscopic mice which do not need to be rolled along a surface but can be moved around in mid air. These are often employed in simulators and game environments where the user doesn't want to be limited to two dimensions.

Touch sensitive screens

Touch screens have been with us for quite a while, but with the advent of smartphones these have really taken off. There are a small number of variants of the touch screen employing different technologies but the most common today uses the change in capacitance to determine which part of the screen has been touched. Capacitative technologies make use of the fact the human finger is an electrical conductor. When a user's finger touches a glass display coated with a transparent conductor it creates a small area of electrical charge whose location can then be identified by suitable software. It is likely that touch screens will become more and more common as the technology in smartphones and personal computers converges.

Scanners

If you want to make use of a printed photograph or some text that is too long to type in, a scanner is a useful piece of technology to have attached to your computer. Modern 2D scanners use a charge coupled device (CCD) or a Contact Image Sensor (CIS) as the image sensor. The mechanism by which these work is sophisticated, but essentially all you need to know at this level is that they are capable of scanning an image in such a fashion that the relevant colour components (red, green and blue) of each pixel of the image can be passed from the scanner to the computer. The software reading the incoming data stream from the scanner will save the data in some appropriate graphic format. Usually these are JPG or TIFF. For more information on these formats take a look at page 76.

If you want your computer to convert the image to text that you can then process in the normal way using your word processor, you'll need something that will read the image file and work out what the pixels making up the letters actually mean. Interpreting the squiggles that make up our letters is called Optical Character Recognition (OCR). These days when you buy a scanner you invariably get a CD or DVD which in addition to the necessary drivers for the scanner will have some programs that will perform OCR for you. To read a piece of text into your computer is usually a simple matter of scanning the document creating an image which the OCR software then interprets as text. The accuracy of the resulting text is very dependent on the resolution of the scanned image. Higher resolutions (300 dots per inch or above) will give you the best results. If too low a resolution is used the software will have difficulty identifying the letters and you'll have to spend quite a bit of time correcting the result.

Output devices

Clearly we need some form of output device to give us the results of our processing of our input data. The most common output devices are described below.

Screens

Screens have been associated with computers pretty much from the very beginning. The first screens were based on cathode ray tubes (CRT) which meant that screens could be as deep as they were wide. Some of these were monsters, extremely heavy and large but with good resolution (i.e. the number of dots or pixels on the screen, large numbers mean higher resolution). Smaller ones were used in early electronic point of sale systems (EPoS systems) and luggable computers such as those by the computer manufacturer Compaq. CRT displays work by firing a 'gun' which emits electrons at a screen which has been coated with phosphor. The impact of the electrons with the phosphor causes the phosphor to light up producing a pixel. The movement of the electrons and hence the image is controlled by means of magnets around the gun. The screens produced X-Rays at relatively small levels but accompanied by high speed flicker and the danger of explosion if the screen were damaged. This meant that when technology advanced to provide us with the liquid crystal display (LCD), CRT screens disappeared rapidly.

LCD displays have many advantages over CRTs. They are far more energy efficient, they do not emit any ionising radiation, are relatively inexpensive and because of the way they work, do not flicker. They are also far smaller, being almost flat and can be made very thin. They work by using the properties of certain crystals suspended in a liquid that are placed between two polarised glass plates. When an electric current is applied to the crystals in a particular area, light is prevented from passing through the glass and the area appears to be black. Modifying the current gives a range of greys. Colour LCDs are created by adding layers for each of red, green and blue. By varying the current at a particular area of the screen on each of the layers it is possible to create various shades of red, green and blue which when combined give us a full range of colours.

Most electronic devices today use some variant of LCD display. Some have astonishing resolutions giving us extremely sharp, realistic images on devices that fit into our pockets.

Printers

Printers have been associated with computer systems from the earliest days. Printer technology has moved on dramatically in the last few years and today colour laser printers are common. Indeed some relatively common colour printers are so well designed that it is possible to print bank notes that to all intensive purposes are indistinguishable from their real counterparts.

The earliest printers of the modern computing era were **dot matrix printers** that worked by hitting a piece of paper, usually on a long roll, with a series of sharp needles pressing against an inked tape. The pressure of the needles made dots on the paper. The combination of dots placed closely together made up a character. With suitable software, text on the screen could be sent as a series of instructions to the printer that made various combinations of needles strike the paper in appropriate positions on the paper. These printers suffered from slow speeds and high levels of noise. Apart from occasional use at some supermarket these printers have disappeared from view.

Next along were **ink jet printers**. They work by firing, or more accurately spitting very small globules of ink out of an array of holes in the ink cartridge onto paper. When an electric current is applied to a small reservoir of ink behind each of the holes the ink is instantly heated up to boiling point and is spat out at high velocity. When ink from colour cartridges (usually yellow, magenta, cyan and black for full colour) is simultaneously spat onto the same point on suitable paper, they merge and produce our full palette of colours.

Ink jet printers can print a range of resolutions, but 1200 or 1440 dots per inch is common. Ink jet printers are relatively inexpensive but on photographic paper they can produce very high quality output and they are relatively fast. Modern versions often provide scanning, photocopying and faxing capabilities in the one package. On the negative side, the ink cartridges are quite expensive to replace and typically hold only small amounts of ink (around 20ml per cartridge). Depending on use, ink cartridges can last typically for between 200 and 600 pages.

Whereas the most popular home printer is almost certainly an ink jet printer due to its relatively light printing load, the business user has much greater printing needs and invariably chooses to use **laser printers**. Initially these were only available in black and white but over recent years colour laser printers have become very popular. These use the science of electrostatics to work. In black and white laser printers, the laser drum is given an overall positive charge and a laser traces out letters and images to be printed on the surface of the drum discharging the area that it shines on. Positively charged toner is then applied to the drum but only attaches to the discharged areas. The drum is then rolled over a sheet of negatively charged paper which pulls the toner off the printer and onto the paper. Finally the paper is passed between heated rollers which fuses the toner with the fibres in the paper resulting in our standard printed copy. This all takes place very rapidly.

Colour laser printers work in exactly the same way as their monochrome brethren but carry out the printing process four times, one for each of cyan, magenta, yellow and black.

As the following questions illustrate, the examiners will want to know that you understand input and output devices in sufficient detail to say what input and output devices might be used in a given application and to describe why the devices you have suggested would be appropriate. There is no need to go into great detail in your answers. Short but accurate descriptions using the correct terminology can give you full marks.

State what is meant by a storage device, an input device and an output device in a computer system. [A451 Jun 2011 Q1 (3)]

- Storage: device used to store data (in binary format for processing later)
- Input: device used to enter data into the computer
- Output: device used to present information as a result of processing to the user

A shopping centre uses several remote-controlled CCTV cameras for security. An operator uses a computer to watch, control and record the output of the cameras. State an input, output and storage device which will be needed by the computer. For each, explain the reason why it is needed. [A451 Jan 2011 Q6 (3,3,3)]

The examiners awarded one mark for stating the device (input, output and storage) and up to two marks per device for explaining why the device was needed. The following list is not exhaustive and other devices that are also valid were awarded marks.

Input device

- Joystick
    - To control the CCTV cameras
    - ...to zoom/tilt/pan
    - ...as they allow precise movements (in 2 axes)
- Keyboard
    - To type commands into the system
    - ...to perform complex control tasks

– Key presses can be used to control the cameras

Output device

- Monitor/Array of monitors
  - Show the output of cameras
  - Showing multiple cameras at a time
- Printer
  - To print hard copy images from the recordings
  - ...e.g. to be used as evidence

Storage device

- Large capacity hard disk drive
  - To record the video feed from all cameras
  - ...simultaneously
  - ...and allowing direct access to any part of the recording
- Rewritable large optical drive or removable flash storage
  - To save recordings (e.g. for a given day)
  - For archiving purposes

Users with Specific needs

Whilst the majority of people who use computers have no special needs, a substantial minority of people do need help in some form or other when using computer systems. For example, some people, often elderly, have some form of visual impairment. Others might have problems with their motor skills, still others might have hearing difficulties. Computer software and in many instances computer hardware, has been designed to cope with such physical impairments. Let's take a look at some of the problems and how computer systems might have been modified to help.

Visual Impairment

For those with a relatively mild visual impairment, i.e. those for whom it is difficult to see the screen, many operating systems will allow the user to increase the size of the fonts used so that the letters are much larger. In addition, icons can be made much bigger and the screen contrast can be increased to make text and images more distinct. It is also possible to provide a means of magnifying text with auditory feedback so that text can be read to the user.

Up to 10% of the population have some form of colour blindness, most of which is relatively mild with the majority having difficulty distinguishing between red and green, whilst others have difficulty distinguishing between yellow and blue. Although very rare, there are some people who have no colour vision and see only in black and white. Software should ensure that colour is not the only way of distinguishing important pieces of information, especially if such colours are red and green or yellow and blue.

For those with more significant visual impairment where perhaps the person is technically blind, screen reader software that reads text out loud to users can be very useful. In order for the user to give instructions to the computer speech voice recognition software can be excellent. Here the user first trains the software to understand their voice, usually by repeating words and phrases provided by the software. Once training is complete, the user has only to speak instructions into a microphone for the computer to understand and respond appropriately. Alternatively, it is possible to connect a braille keyboard to a computer so that the user can type instructions via braille.

Motor impairments

For some users it might be difficult or perhaps impossible to use a mouse or a keyboard. For such users other input devices might be more appropriate, for example tracker balls or switches and joysticks. Again, speech recognition software can be very useful here. Perhaps the most well known example of a user with motor impairment is Professor Stephen Hawking who has motor neurone disease and uses a combination of these technologies. He has a motorised wheelchair equipped with specially written software to allow him to move around.

Hearing problems

Some users have problems with their hearing. For these users, a useful technique is to convert speech automatically into captions which the users can then read. For users with normal hearing, there are situations where this is very useful, for example in factories where the noise level is often very high.

A secondary school wants the computer systems to be more accessible to students with disabilities. Describe, with examples, input

and output devices which are available for students with disabilities. The quality of written communication will be assessed in your answer to this question. [A451 Jun 2011 Q1 (6)]

The examiners were looking for you to make the following points.

- Input devices:

  - Puff-suck switch: allows mobility impaired users to control e.g. clicking a mouse, by sucking or blowing through a tube
  - Simplified/concept keyboards e.g. for Braille, or larger keys
  - Eye tracking input – Camera is used to follow the users eye movements and use these to control e.g. movement of mouse on screen

- Output device:

  - Braille printer – print documents on paper in braille as raised bumps. Some braillers have plastic bumps which can be raised or lowered by software, so output does not have to be on paper
  - Text to speech
  - Screen magnifiers

2.5 SECONDARY STORAGE

Secondary storage refers to storage that will retain information even when power is removed from the system.

Why do we need it?

When the computer is first switched on there are no instructions in RAM for the CPU to read. Instead (as explained on page 21) instructions are read initially from ROM. After checking that the system is fit for purpose, subsequent instructions making up the operating system will need to be brought into RAM from secondary storage, usually, but not necessarily off the hard disk. Later when the user wants to browse the Internet or read her email, applications will need to be brought into the RAM off secondary storage. Finally, after writing a document a user would usually want to save the result of his or her hard work and again some form of secondary storage is necessary.

Common storage technologies

Hard Disk Drive

The most common form of storage technology is the probably the hard disk drive. This is a magnetic form of storage where data is stored in the form of magnetised patterns. It was invented in the early 1950s and whilst the early drives were extremely large and heavy weighing many kilograms, stored only a few megabytes of data at best and cost many thousands of pounds, modern drives weigh a few hundred grammes, can store terabytes of data and cost only a few tens of pounds.

The hard disk is actually made up of a number of disks each of which is used to store data on both upper and lower surfaces. Data is stored in the form of tiny magnetised regions called magnetic domains. These domains have an orientation (a direction) parallel and horizontal to the disk and whereas a zero bit might be represented by a direction parallel to the disk, a bit 1 will be represented by the direction horizontal to the disk surface. Data is organised into **sectors** which normally hold 512 bytes of data and **clusters** usually representing 8 sectors, i.e. $512 \times 8 = 4096$ bits on a series of concentric tracks. Outer tracks are clearly longer than inner tracks, but all hold the same amount of data. Disks are stacked one above the other. Data is written and read to and from each of the disks via a read/write device called a 'head'. Each surface spins rapidly beneath its own head.

When an application asks the operating system to save some data, the read-/write head is instructed to move to a track where there is a free sector (i.e. a sector which is currently not storing any data). The time that the head takes to move into position is called the **seek** time and is typically between 10 and 20 milliseconds. Once above the sector the head must wait until the spinning disk causes a free sector to come into position underneath the head. The time taken for this to happen is called the **latency** of the disk and the faster the disk is spinning, the shorter the latency period. Once in position, the data is written to the disk at a rate of 5 to 40 Mbytes per second (the **data rate**).

Similarly, if the application is attempting to retrieve a file, the read/write head is instructed to move to the the sector which holds the start of the file. Once above the sector, the head must wait until the spinning disk causes the correct sector to appear underneath the head. Once in position the data is quickly read off the sector and sent to the application.

To summarise, hard disks are used to store the operating system, applications, user files and pretty much anything you can think of.

USB memory sticks

USB memory sticks use a form of long term storage called **flash memory** integrated with a USB (Universal Serial Bus) connector. Flash memory is a specific form of EEPROM (electrically erasable programmable read-only memory) that can as its name suggests be erased and re-programmed electrically. The read-only part of the name refers to the fact that once programmed it is read-only until electrically erased. This form of long term storage is extremely robust, very fast, (though not as fast as RAM), very cheap and is available in very small packages. It replaces the floppy disk, a form of magnetic storage device that in its original form in the 1980s, held 80 kBytes of data. Its modern counterpart is perfectly capable of storing 256 GBytes of data, though such large capacities are at the moment still quite expensive. Smaller capacities of 16 GB and 32 GB are very much cheaper and are in common use.

USB memory sticks are most often used to store user files, though with such large capacities available for such little cost they can also be used to store and move large numbers of images, sound files and video.

Solid State Drives

Solid State Drives (SSD) are data storage devices that are starting to replace hard disk drives in some high end computer systems. Using solid state technology in the form of a sophisticated flash drive, unlike hard disks they have no moving parts and are thus far less susceptible to shocks. SSDs have lower latency and access times and are thus quite a bit quicker than hard disks. However, they are currently quite expensive. At the time of writing, 160 Gbyte SSD drives are retailing for roughly the same price as 4 TBytes of hard disk storage. You can however expect them to get considerably cheaper as demand grows.

SSDs have additional advantages over hard disk drives in that they are silent, they take considerably less power and are therefore attractive to laptop manufacturers.

Optical storage systems

Optical storage systems in the form of CDs and DVDs are common in modern computer systems. Digital data is encoded as tiny pits or bumps in the surface of the disk. Each pit or bump represents a 1 whilst the lack of a pit or bump at a particular point indicates a 0. Disks are commonly 12 cm in diameter, though larger disks up to 30 cm are also used. To read data, a disk reader spins the disk at up to 4,000 rpm and a laser is shone onto the surface of the disk. The mirrored surface of the disk reflects the laser light and can be read by suitable optoelectronic hardware which can distinguish between light that has been reflected from the pits and bumps and that which has been reflected back from a flat surface, thus discriminating between a 1 and a 0.

CD and DVD disks are available in a variety of formats. Data and music CDs have the digital data encoded on polycarbonate plastic at the time of manufacture. The plastic is then covered with a very thin aluminium layer. These disks cannot be written to by the user.

CD-R and DVD-R disks replace the aluminium layer with an organic dye compound. When heated by the laser to a specific temperature the dye is 'burned' a darker colour than the rest of the dye. Laser light reflected from this tiny burnt spot indicates a 1 at that position. By focussing the laser precisely at a series of points as the disk is rotated beneath the laser, a pattern of 1s and 0s can be encoded. This process cannot be reversed, so CD-R and DVD-R disks are write once, read many disks.

CD-RW and DVD-RW use a different technology. The aluminium layer is replaced with a special alloy of indium, antimony, silver and tellurium which exhibits a phase change when heated. The normally crystalline form of the alloy darkens when heated to around 700 °C. When heated to around 200 °C the alloy returns to its normal crystalline state and the dark spot disappears. When data is to be written to such a disk, the disk is spun and the laser heated to 700 °C. When a 1 is to be written the laser is shone onto the disk and a tiny dark spot is the result. By switching the laser on and off very rapidly, a series of 1s and 0s can be written to the disk. To erase, the laser is heated to 200 °C and shone onto the disk. All 1s are then re-written as 0s. Software then remembers that this section of the disk is now free to be written at some future date.

CDs typically store 800 MBytes, whilst a single sided, single layer DVD can store 4.7 GBytes, i.e. roughly 2 hours of video. A double sided, dual layer

DVD can store up to 17 GBytes. Single layer Blu-ray DVDs can hold 25 GBytes whilst dual layer Blu-ray DVDs can hold 50 GBytes of data. To put this into perspective, a dual layer Blu-ray DVD can hold 9 hours of high definition (HD) video, or around 23 hours of standard definition (SD) video.

You are not required to know the technical details of these storage technologies, but as with input and output devices, the examiners will expect you to use your knowledge of storage devices to recommend and describe suitable storage devices for a given scenario. The following questions are typical.

A secondary school is upgrading its computer equipment. Complete the table below to show whether magnetic, optical or solid state storage is most appropriate for each of the following uses. Give a reason for each case. The first one has been done for you. [A451 Jun 2011 Q1 (6)]

Use	Magnetic, optical or solid state	Reason why this is most appropriate
Storing pictures in a camera	solid state	Is not affected by the camera moving around
Handheld device used by students for field work		
Storage drives on the school's main server		
Videos of the school production to be given to parents		

Answer

Use	Magnetic, optical or solid state	Reason why this is most appropriate
Storing pictures in a camera	solid state	Is not affected by the camera moving around
Handheld device used by students for field work	solid state	Quick access (for instant on)/not sensitive to being moved around while used
Storage drives on the school's main server	magnetic	Very Large capacity/relatively cheap
Videos of the school production to be given to parents	optical	Cheap/Portable/Universally readable by most computers and dedicated video disc players

Davinder is a music student. She needs to take her files from her home computer into college. Identify a method of storage which is suitable for taking her music files into college. State why this method is suitable. [A451 Specimen Paper 2010 Q7 (2)]

- Flash storage/USB stick/MP3 player
  - small and convenient to carry
  - plug and play
- Optical storage / CD-ROM / CD-RW
  - convenient to carry / cheap
  - music can be stored in a format which can be played by e.g. HiFis.
- External hard drive
  - plug and play on either computer
  - and a large capacity for music files

The table below contains a list of hardware devices. Tick one box in each row to show what type of device it is. The first one has been done for you. [A451 Specimen Paper 2010 Q1 (4)]

Hardware device	Input	Output	Processing	Storage	Communication
Monitor		✓			
CPU					
Mouse					
DVD-Drive					
Speakers					

Answer:

Hardware device	Input	Output	Processing	Storage	Communication
Monitor		✓			
CPU			✓		
Mouse	✓				
DVD-Drive				✓	
Speakers		✓			

Software

Hardware is important, but without software it is simply inert junk. Hardware with software can take you to the moon and (hopefully) back again. It makes the Internet work, it flies aeroplanes, manages the world's financial systems, manufactures our cars, decodes the human genome and can make great coffee. Software comes in various guises.

3.1 THE OPERATING SYSTEM

The operating system is probably the most important piece of software on your computer. You may think that you can't live without your music library or the latest role playing game, but without the operating system your music library won't be able to access the hard disk which holds the binary information that represents your music collection nor will it be able to send the information to the speakers for you to listen to it. Similarly without an operating system, the amazing graphics of your favourite computer game won't be displayed on your screen, nor will you be able to get input from your keyboard or mouse.

So, as a first approximation, the operating system controls the hardware. It relays information to and from application software such as internet browsers, word processors, games and music players to the hardware.

Let me give you a practical example. Suppose that you have just written a letter using your favourite word processor and you now want to print the letter. You click **Print**, a dialogue box appears, you select the printer and press **Enter** The document is sent to the printer. It works. Unbeknown to you, your word processor has no idea how to talk to the printer. In fact it doesn't know whether there is a printer attached at all. What it does know is how to ask the operating system for help. When you click **Print**, the word processor tells the operating system that it wants to print and hands it the data it wants printed. The operating system then produces the dialogue box and gives you a selection of printers (that is if you have more than one). You select one and the operating system sends the data to the printer.

There's even more to it than that. How did you select the word processor in the first place? By clicking on an icon, or selecting it from a menu?

User Interface

The operating system provides you with your user interface. Your entire interaction with the computer is controlled by the operating system. All icons and menus outside of the those shown within an application are provided by the operating system. In fact, all key presses and mouse clicks and movements at all times are tracked, stored and passed on to applications by the operating system.

There are a variety of user interfaces that you will come into contact with at some point. The Windows, Icons, Menus and Pointers (WIMP) interface that is an integral part of your experience of using a computer system running Microsoft Windows, the Apple Mac OS X or Linux represents what we call a Graphical User Interface or GUI for short. These interfaces provide rectangular sections of the screen which we call 'windows' for your applications to show themselves, icons which you click on to start applications, menus which provide a simple way of providing you with alternatives and pointers commonly in the form of an arrow which represents the movement of the mouse on screen.

The GUI interface is a little over 25 years old. Apple introduced the Macintosh with a GUI interface on January 24th 1984. Microsoft brought out Windows version 1.0 on November 20th 1985. Prior to that computers were controlled from what are called **command line** interfaces whereby the user issued a string of commands as a single line of text. There were no graphics, no images, just green (or sometimes amber) text on a black background. Command line interfaces still exist today and are often the interface of choice for computer scientists who want complete control of their computer system.

Early mobile phones were an excellent example of a menu driven user interface. These phones provided the user with a small set of buttons which when pressed selected a menu. Further button presses allowed the user to select from a small list of menu options including the option to select another menu.

In this way, users could 'drill' down the menu structure to select the option they wanted. Today's smartphones provide a GUI interface often every bit as good as its desktop brethren with windows, icons, menus and pointers replaced with a touch screen interface.

Memory Management

In addition to providing a user interface, the operating system needs to manage memory. What memory? Well, first off it needs to manage the RAM. All applications and the operating system itself has to be in RAM because that's where the CPU looks for its instructions. Once the boot process is finished, and the operating system is sitting in RAM, the first thing the user normally does is to start running applications. These need to be copied from the hard disk by the operating system and put into RAM. Clearly you don't want the applications to overlap each other. The operating system takes care of this by carefully placing each application into its own memory space, complete with its own data area. The operating system also manages when each application runs and it makes sure that no application can write or read from the memory area of other applications. Each application has its own area of RAM that is reserved solely for its own use and that no other application can damage in any way.

Additionally, the operating system takes care of virtual memory. See page 24 to remind yourself what that means.

Peripheral Management

In addition to providing users with some means of using the computer and managing memory, the operating system manages access to all peripherals attached to the computer system such as printers, cameras and speakers. When an application wants to print a document, it hands over the data to the operating system which then sends the appropriate instructions and the relevant data to the printer. The application itself has no knowledge of what printer is attached or whether indeed any printer is attached.

You may have noticed that once you've told the system to print, you can continue working on your document, whilst the operating system takes care of the actual printing process. This is possible because the operating system is able to multi-task (see the next next section for more information on multi-tasking). Similarly when an application wants to save a file, the file is handed over to the operating system. The operating system sends instructions to whichever long term storage device the user wishes to use and then streams the data in the file to the device. The operating system then updates its list of file names and where on the long term storage device the file is stored, so that later, when the user wants to retrieve the file, the operating system knows where the file has been stored.

When a new device such as a camera or printer is connected to the computer, software appropriate to the device has to be installed before the device can be used. This software is called a **device driver** and after installation it effectively becomes part of the operating system so that any application that needs to communicate with the device can then do so. Modern operating systems have an extensive set of device drivers already installed so that installation is achieved by simply connecting the device to the computer system.

Multi-tasking

Multi-tasking is the ability of your computer system to run more than one application apparently simultaneously. I say apparently because the CPU can only execute one instruction at a time. In modern dual and quad core CPUs, each core can indeed execute instructions at the same time as other cores, but each core has to fetch its instruction from the same memory, access the same graphic card and write to the hard disk, so to say that more than one application is running at the same time is only partially true. Dual and quad core CPUs aside, CPUs can only execute one instruction at a time, which means that if the CPU is running an instruction from say the set of instructions that make up your internet browser it cannot at the same time be running your email client. It might appear to you that it is doing both at the same time, but that's simply because the CPU is switching between applications much too quickly for you to notice that it is happening.

The simplest multi-tasking algorithm is called the **Round Robin** whereby all tasks that need to run are held by the operating system in a list. Each task on the list is given perhaps 3ms of CPU time before it is halted and the next task in the list is given its turn. Once all tasks on the list have had their turn, the operating system starts again with the first task on the list.

More complex algorithms might allocate priorities to tasks. If the operating system regards one or more tasks as more important than others it might run the task more frequently or it might run it for longer each time it had its turn. With some operating systems it is possible for the user to re-allocate priorities so that a particular task is given more time to run.

Operating systems such as Windows, OS X and Linux have many tasks in the list, most of which are dormant and are only activated if something happens that is relevant to the task. For example, a computer may be connected to others on a network. The task that handles data entering or leaving the computer via the network port only needs to run when data is waiting to come in or it is asked to send data by an application program. The operating system takes care of this and only puts tasks in the list that actually need to run.

Single and multi-user

When an operating system only allows one person at a time to use a computer system, we say that the operating system is **single-user**. When an operating system allows many people apparently simultaneous access to a computer system, we say that the operating system is **multi-user**. Multi-user access is achieved in a very similar way to multi-tasking. Each person is placed in a list and given access in turn to the resources of the computer system for a few milliseconds at a time. Once everyone has had their precious few milliseconds the whole process is repeated. Most modern operating systems are multi-user and multi-tasking which means that many people can run many tasks apparently simultaneously on the same computer system.

Security

All operating systems have security mechanisms in place for keeping potential intruders locked out of the computer. You will have already experienced something of this in school where you will be required to log in to your computer, giving your username and password before the system will allow you to use the system at all. Having logged in, there are additional levels of security. For example, although you are probably able to change the background screen image and move your icons around the screen, you may not be able to install software and you most certainly are unlikely to be allowed to add or delete users from the system. The operating system manages this by providing various levels of security. The most powerful user is usually referred to as the **administrator**. He or she is able to do pretty much anything they like, but they are likely to be highly experienced, fully qualified system engineers who know what they are doing.

On some operating systems there are further distinctions made between power users and ordinary users. Power users are given more privileges. For

example, they may be allowed to install some types of software or add printers, whereas ordinary users are often strictly restricted in what they can and
cannot do.

**One of the functions of an operating system is multi-tasking. Ex-
plain one reason why multi-tasking is needed in an operating system.** [A451 Jan 2012 Q2 (2)]

- It allows more than one program to run (apparently) at he same time
- ... by sharing processor time and resources between the programs
- It enables the user to be more productive
- ... e.g. cut text from a document and paste it into an email

State two other functions of an operating system. (2)

- Provides a user interface
- Provides a platform for applications to run
- Handles memory management
- Does file and disk management
- Does Peripheral management and provides a platform for hardware

**Ali's new computer uses a single-user, multi-tasking operating sys-
tem. What is a single-user operating system?** [A451 Specimen Paper
2010 Q5 (2)]

- Only one user
- ... can use the computer at any given time

What is a multi-tasking operating system? (2)

- The computer can (appear to) run several programs
- ... at the same time
- E.g. word processing while playing music

Common utility programs

All modern operating systems include a variety of programs that perform a
range of useful functions. These programs are called utility programs and
they include such programs as anti-Virus, firewalls, formatting and fragmentation tools. In the next few sections we shall take a closer look at some of
these.

Anti-Virus

The Internet has brought to us almost unlimited access to information but whereas today we are connected to the Internet, it should not be forgotten that the Internet is now connected to us with data flowing in both directions. Each time we send a message onto the Internet asking for some piece of information, perhaps a web page, perhaps a song or a film, the web page, song and film are returned to us. If we are not careful, unbeknown to us they may carry additional data in the form of software which is designed to attack our computer systems. Additional data of this type is called by a variety of names depending on its function. If it simply wants to monitor what we do it is called **spyware**. If it intends to damage our computer or to hide for a while before preparing to attack other computers it is called a **virus**, a **worm**, or a **trojan**.

A number of companies have produced software whose job it is to detect, prevent and destroy such programs. On modern multi-tasking operating systems anti-virus software runs as a background task constantly monitoring incoming data from the Internet and looking for tell-tale signs of infection. Unfortunately, it's not terribly difficult to write a virus and consequently each year many hundreds of new viruses are released onto the Internet and every year many tens of thousands of computers are infected.

It is always advisable to run some form of anti-virus software, simply because it is very easy to become infected. It is true that some sites may be more likely to infect you than others, but since it's not difficult to attach infected programs to data on almost any site, it is perfectly possible to become infected from the most innocuous sites.

Spyware

Whereas viruses, trojans and worms are usually intended to do serious damage to computer systems, spyware is designed to spy on a user's activity on the internet. It will typically keep track of which web sites are visited for its own commercial purposes. For example, if the spyware notices that the user often visits game sites, it can inform its creators of this and they in turn can sell the user's personal details on to a third party company that targets people who like games. The user, unaware of what has happened, is surprised by suddenly receiving an increased supply of junk mail relating to games.

Spyware may have much more serious consequences however. Some spyware will watch a user's key strokes in an effort to find usernames and passwords for online banking services. Having collected the relevant information, it is then perfectly possible for them to pretend to be the user and to take money from the user's personal bank account. It can be very difficult to convince the bank that they should return the missing cash. These situations can become even more unpleasant if a wide range of personal information has been accessed. In such circumstances the user's very identity has been stolen and it can be extraordinarily difficult, very expensive and take a great deal of time to retrieve a stolen identity.

Anti-spyware and anti-virus software are often combined in a single package which protects the user from both spyware and viruses, but an alternative solution is to install both anti-virus and anti-spyware packages, often from companies which specialise in one but not the other.

Firewalls

Firewalls are designed to prevent 'hackers' gaining entry into your computer from the Internet. To understand what firewalls do, some background information is required.

All traffic on the Internet is sent in small packets of data, typically around 1,500 bytes (1.5 K Bytes) in size. Larger pieces of information such as music downloads and emails are chopped up into smaller packet sized chunks which then find their own way across the Internet. Each packet contains the address where it is coming from and the address where it is going to. Addresses are currently 32 bits long, i.e. four bytes and since each byte can hold a number between 0 and 255 these addresses, called Internet Protocol (IP) addresses, are often written in the form 167.223.1.76 where each number is in the range 0 – 255 and separated by single dots.

Each computer connected to the Internet **must** have a unique address otherwise no computer system will be able to send packets to them. In addition much like countries have ports through which flow food, machinery and people, computer operating systems use the same idea for data flowing into and out of the computer. Computer systems also call these ports. In the UK we have ports such as Dover, Harwich and Liverpool. Computers have 65,536 ports but these are numbered not named. Most ports can be used for any purpose, but some ports have been given special functions. For example web servers listening to requests from users usually listen on port 80. Email is usually sent out of port 25 whereas incoming email is usually received on port 110.

Firewalls monitor packets coming and going on these ports. The most restrictive firewalls close all ports so that nothing can move in or out of the computer. Most firewalls will open up a few common ports so that for instance users can email, browse the web and download music, but the remaining ports will all be closed. The popular massive, multi-user, online, role playing game (MMORPG) World of Warcraft needs ports 3174, 6112 and 6881 opened so that it can download patches to the game. Other games might ask for other ports to be opened.

Hackers trying to get into a computer system will run special software called a port scanner which will rapidly send data to all ports in an effort to see which are open. If the software finds an open port it will try to access the operating system perhaps to take over the computer, perhaps simply to look around. In neither case is this desirable.

In the continual battle against hackers, firewalls are an incredibly important weapon. Most routers attached to the external telephone or cable line have their own sophisticated firewalls but as a further precaution a secondary firewall can run on your own personal computer. This is probably overkill, but some people like the added security.

Formatting

The principal job of any storage system and one of the main tasks of any operating system is to allow the user to store and retrieve information. However, before storage devices can be used they need to be **formatted**. Formatting prepares the storage device for first use. It creates an empty file system on the hard disk, complete with sectors and tracks and very importantly, uses some of the sectors, usually on the first few tracks on the device, to create an empty list called the **File Allocation Table (FAT)**. The FAT is used to keep track of where data has been stored and to keep track of any damaged areas of the disk to ensure that they will not be used when data is later saved.

You may have seen crime dramas in which computers owned by a suspected criminal have been taken as evidence. Although the suspect may have deleted any incriminating data from the hard disk, somehow the police are able to recover the information. This scenario is perfectly plausible because when you delete data, you are in fact merely recording the fact (i.e. modifying the FAT) that the space used by your data is now available. The data itself is not removed which means that unless the data is later overwritten, it remains intact and perfectly readable.

File Transfer

All data is stored in the form of **files**. In simple terms, a file is simply a collection of data organised in some sensible way. Documents, spreadsheets, web pages, pictures and music are all saved as files of data each with their own unique file structure. This structure needs to be preserved when stored.

During the formatting process, the operating system creates **sectors** on the storage device. A sector is only 512 bytes in size which is quite small. Consequently sectors are grouped into larger units called **clusters** which are typically 4096 bytes in size. Most files are much larger than this which means that when they are in the process of being stored, files are 'chopped' into cluster size pieces and placed onto the storage medium in the most convenient locations. The location of the first cluster of each file is stored in the FAT together with additional information such as where the following cluster for the file can be found.

The FAT is an example of what we call a **linked list**. Each link in the chain points to where the next link is. When a file is retrieved, the operating system reads the FAT, finds the location of the first cluster, reads it to find the location of the second cluster and so on until all clusters are found. As the linked list is read, data is copied off the storage device and into RAM.

When the operating system wishes to write a file, it first reads the FAT to find a list of available free clusters. If sufficient space is available it begins copying data from RAM to the first free cluster on the storage device. When that is full a second free cluster is identified, its address is recorded in the linked list and data is stored. This continues until all the file is copied to the storage device.

When files are transferred from one location to another it is not necessary to physically move the data on the hard disk. It is sufficient simply to update the FAT with the new location information; the physical data does not need to move.

Defragmentation

Defragmentation is the process whereby the operating system is given an opportunity to 're-arrange' where on the storage device files are stored so as to optimise storing and retrieval time. Files are read into RAM, cluster by cluster and then written back to the storage device to new cluster addresses. The linked list is updated and the process continues until all, or as many files as possible have been relocated into more efficient positions on the storage device.

The reason why some storage devices, hard disks in particular, need to be defragmented is that when a hard disk is new, the operating system is able to choose exactly which of the clusters available is chosen for a particular file to maximise efficient reading and writing. Hard disks have mechanical read/write heads and as the disk spins beneath them, they move backwards and forwards over the hard disk reading and writing data. The combination of spinning and lateral movement of the heads mean that there is an optimal way of storing and retrieving information. Over time, as free space is used up, files are saved and files are deleted, it is no longer possible for the operating system to pick and choose precisely where it stores new files. The result is that reading and writing to the storage device will take longer and as the files become more and more fragmented this slowing down becomes more and more noticeable.

Some storage devices are particularly prone to fragmentation. Hard disks are one of these and depending on usage levels it is advisable to defragment a hard drive perhaps once a year for moderate use. Flash memory is very much quicker than hard disks so defragmentation is rarely if ever necessary.

System Maintenance

All computer systems whatever their design or origin require regular maintenance to ensure that performance over time doesn't degrade. As we saw earlier, it is possible to improve storage device read and write access times by defragmentation. Additionally, since, despite the best intentions of the programmers, any piece of software has some bugs in it somewhere, software companies spend much of their time addressing such bugs. They release bug fixes and enhancements to their software products on a regular basis. Operating systems can never be free of bugs and regular updates are made available across the web.

System Information and Diagnosis

To check whether your system is performing as well as you might like it is possible to track its performance over time by running a suite of diagnostic software on a regular basis. This type of software will tell you how quickly the hard disk is reading and writing data, how much disk space is left, how well the graphics card is performing and how memory is being used. All operating systems have a suite of diagnostic software available and it is a good idea to run these occasionally to see how a system is performing. At any instant, the operating system will have a considerable number of tasks running. These tasks perform a range of useful functions, including background printing, network monitoring, keyboard and mouse monitoring, applications that are currently in use and many others.

However, some tasks are unnecessary and it is advisable to remove them from memory and ideally from ever starting up. Depending on the operating system, there are a range of diagnostic tools which explains what each of the tasks currently in memory are, what they do and whether they are needed. Cutting down on unnecessary tasks can improve the performance of a computer system considerably.

System Cleanup Tools

An operating system such as Microsoft Windows has spawned a range of software tools to help clean up a computer system. These range from the diagnostic tools described above which will help remove unwanted tasks, to tools that will remove unnecessary temporary files from the system and remove and clean up the registry settings. Each application that is installed under Microsoft Windows is obliged to register itself with the registry (essentially a large database stored on the hard drive). Registration involves adding itself to the registry and writing a range of configuration options to the registry file. As programs are installed the registry will grow and grow and since applications read their configuration settings from the registry file on startup, the larger the file, the slower they will start. Other cleanup tools will find and remove spyware and adware from the computer.

Automatic Updating

Regular updating of software is a very good thing. It is particularly important to update the operating system regularly. Companies such as Microsoft and Apple are constantly fixing bugs and improving their operating systems and their application software. It is very sensible to check regularly to see whether updates have been released. To help with that process and to make sure that systems are updated regularly, most operating systems have some form of automatic updating process. On a regular basis the automated process will make contact with the operating system manufacturer to check if updates are available. If new updates are available, it will download and install them automatically.

Describe the two following types of common utility programs, Antivirus and Disk defragmenter [A451 Jun 2011 Q5 (2,2)]

Antivirus:

- Scans the computer periodically
- ...to check if any software has been installed which contains code that may harm the computer
- Removes and/or quarantines these programs and notifies the user
- Prevents these programs from being installed
- Protects the computer by preventing important files (e.g. the boot sector or operating system) from being changed

Disk defragmenter:

- Moves (parts of) files around so that all parts of a file are stored together (allowing files to be accessed more quickly)
- Free space is collected together (allowing large files to be saved easily)

Ali wants to know which utility programs he will need to keep his computer secure and running smoothly. Discuss the utility programs Ali will need, justifying why he needs them. [A451 Specimen Paper 2010 Q5 (6)]

As with all questions of this type and where the quality of your written answer is being assessed it is important to think carefully about the question before preparing your answer. In this particular question you will need to think about what utility programs help with security and what utility programs help to keep your computer running smoothly. There is no set answer but the examiners were looking for answers that included the following points.

Security:

- Anti-virus and Anti-spyware should be installed that regularly checks the computer for programs that are designed to harm the system. These programs gather information about viruses and spyware and deletes or disables them. Viruses and spyware are easily acquired from the Internet and could result in significant damage and financial loss, for example identity theft, if not removed.

- Firewall - this controls access to the computer through the network and is used to prevent hackers from gaining access to the computer
- Anti-virus and anti-spyware programs need to be updated regularly, because new viruses and spyware programs are produced all the time

To keep the computer running smoothly:

- Disk maintenance
  - Defragmenting. This reorganises files so that they are stored in blocks at the most appropriate points on the hard drive. This means that file access is quicker and it may free up space
  - Disk cleanup. Regularly search for and delete files which are no longer needed, because this frees up space which can be used for other programs
- System maintenance
  - System cleanup. The computer is searched for programs and settings which are no longer needed – these may be slowing the computer down and removing them can improve system performance
  - System update. Search the Internet for updated versions of software on the computer and download and install the updates. This ensures that the computer always has the latest version including any fixes for known problems or security issues

3.2 SOFTWARE TYPES

Software comes in many shapes and guises. There is the **operating system** which does pretty much everything on computer systems. Often installed after the operating system, but once installed then forming part of it are the **device drivers** - software that allow the computer to read, write and control external hardware devices such as graphics cards, printers, cameras and a whole host of other esoteric devices.

After these comes the **applications**. These are programs which let the user do something useful, such as browse the Internet, write a letter, prepare a presentation or send email. They use the operating system to talk to the keyboard, the screen, the hard disk, the printer and any other external hardware device. Whereas the operating system runs quietly in the background, minding its own business it's the applications that get all the attention. Most users are unaware of the operating system since they spend most if not all of their time interacting with applications. Applications can be divided into three main categories.

Proprietary Software

Proprietary applications, often called 'off the shelf' software are created by software companies as commercial products. Examples of these are games such as World of Warcraft from Blizzard, office applications such as Word and Excel by Microsoft, web design tools such as Dreamweaver from Adobe and mathematics software such as Mathematica from Wolfram Research. All of these applications are highly sophisticated programs, the result of many thousands of man years (one man working for a year = one man year) of effort.

These products usually arrive in nice shiny boxes with extensive documentation, on-line customer and technical support, training courses and a whole host of web pages devoted to helping people master their complexities. They are inexpensive in comparison to the money spend in creating, maintaining and enhancing them.

Custom Written (Bespoke) Software

Custom written applications, often referred to as **bespoke applications** are programs that are created for a particular user by a software company and are designed to do whatever the particular customer wants and to do it well. Customers often have very specific needs and requirements and 'off-the-shelf' software simply isn't good enough. This route can be extremely expensive, and contracts running into many hundreds of thousands of pounds are common. The British Government has gone down this route on many occasions, commissioning billions of pounds worth of custom written software from its suppliers. The advantages of such an approach are that when finished the software should do exactly what the customer wants on the hardware that is used. Disadvantages are numerous. Apart from the expense, which is often horrendous in the case of government contracts, many projects simply fail to complete either because they were badly specified or because they turned out to be too complex to build or the requirements changed.

Open Source Software

Open source software has a variety of meanings but essentially it means that the source code, i.e. the software that is actually written by programmers is made freely available. Anyone is allowed to download the source and if they are skilled enough they can test it, edit it, improve it and send their improvements back to the computer scientists who are currently maintaing the software (often the original authors of the program). If their changes provide genuine enhancements to the original program their improvements are added to subsequent releases. In this way the software improves continuously, supported by potentially many thousands of highly skilled software engineers all over the world.

Open source software powers the Internet. The overwhelming majority of web pages are distributed by an open source web server called Apache, as is most of the software that is used to build web pages. Firefox (an internet browser), Java, (a language found on computer platforms world wide) and Linux (the Unix-based operating system started by a young postgraduate student in Finland) are all examples of extremely successful open source projects.

There are a number of advantages of open source amongst which are that customers can get highly sophisticated and well supported software at next to no cost. However, the software often has to be customised in order to perform the specific task that a customer wants performed and it may be difficult and possibly quite expensive to find someone capable of performing the necessary customisation. Additionally, some projects are quite small and may prove to be poorly supported with little or no documentation.

A school uses a computer system to monitor the attendance, punctuality and homework of its pupils. The school has decided to use off-the-shelf software. State two advantages of off-the-shelf software. [A451 Jan 2012 Q7 (2)]

- Available now so the school will not have to wait
- Recommendations are available and it can been seen working in other schools
- Tried and tested and less likely to contain bugs (given how critical the application is)
- Costs less than custom-written as the school does not pay for the full cost of development
- More (third party) support and documentation

State two disadvantages of off-the-shelf software. (2)

- May contain features which the school does not need
- May not contain features which the school needs
- May not be compatible with school's hardware
- May not be compatible with school's processes
- The developer is not available to make adjustments necessary

A shopkeeper needs software to manage the accounts of her shop. She decides to use off-the-shelf software instead of custom written software. Describe two advantages to the shopkeeper of off-the-shelf software, compared to custom written software. [A451 Specimen Paper 2012 Q3 (2,2)]

- It is immediately available
- ...so the shopkeeper can start using it straightaway
- It is tried and tested
- ...and so less likely to have errors
- There are no development costs
- ...as this has already been borne by the developer
- More support is available since there are
- ...many other users who can provide help/third party help books, help lines or web sites

Karen wants to use handheld computers to take customers orders in her restaurant. She is thinking of using custom written, open source software. State what is meant by custom written software. [A451 Jan 2011 Q5 (1)]

- Software created especially for a user, in this case Karen's restaurant

State two reasons why Karen may decide to use custom written software. (2)

- Appropriate software may not exist
- Existing software may not do exactly what restaurant wants
- Existing software may not be compatible with the restaurant's hardware
- Existing software may contain additional features (and be more complex and expensive)

Discuss the implications of creating open source software for the restaurant. The quality of written communication will be assessed in your answer to this question. (6)

As with all questions that assess the quality of your written communication, take some time to think through the points you want to make before you start answering the question. In this particular question you should give some thought to what sort of implications are the examiners thinking of. The software is open source so what are the implications of using open source rather than using commercial software. Is the software likely to be of higher quality or lower? Is it likely to be more reliable? Is getting the source code useful? Is Karen likely to want software written specifically for her available to her competitors? What sort of support is available with open source? Is open source morally superior? These are the sorts of things you should consider before answering and when you do so, write carefully and make your points clearly.

The examiners were expecting the following points to be made.

- Open source – this means that it is licence-free, and the restaurant will then make the software and its source code available for others to use and possibly improve
- There are financial implications which means that there is no need to pay for the license, Karen can reuse and adapt free open source software which is similar BUT development is going to cost something and the software will be available to competitors
- Quality implications include: large community of open source developers can see and comment on code or can be consulted/ software has to conform to certain standards to be released under public licence BUT open source code is used as is, with no guarantees,
- Ethical implications include: open source encourages open culture values - free sharing, collaboration BUT the restaurant is a business trying to make a profit

4

Representation of data in computer systems

4.1 UNITS

Bits, Nibbles and Bytes

Humans are decimal counting machines. We have 10 fingers (including our thumbs) which is probably why we have only ten symbols, 0, 1, 2, 3, 4, 5, 6, 7, 8 and 9 to represent numbers.

Computers are binary counting machines. They make use of only two symbols, 0 and 1. Each of these is called a **bit**. If we put four of them together in a group such as 1001 we call this a **nibble**. If we put eight of them together in a group such as 10001001 we call this a **byte**.

A bit can therefore hold one of two numbers. Either it holds a 0 or it holds a 1.

A nibble (4 bits) can hold one of 2^4, i.e. sixteen different numbers, ranging from 0000 to 1111.

A byte (8 bits) can hold one of $2^8 = 256$ numbers, ranging from 00000000 to 11111111.

Bytes are used extensively throughout computing to represent the size of things. One byte can be used to hold a single character, such as the letter 'a' or '+'. 1024 bytes is called a kilobyte (KB) and 1024 kilobytes, i.e. $1024 \times 1024 = 1,048,576$ bytes is called a megabyte (MB).

1024 megabytes is called a Gigabyte (GB) and 1024 gigabytes is called a terabyte (TB). A terabyte therefore holds $1024 \times 1024 \times 1024 \times 1024 = 2^{40} = 1,099,511,627,776$ bytes. The next table summaries this information.

59

1 bit	=	a single digit, 0 or 1
4 bits	=	1 nibble
8 bits	=	1 byte
1024 bytes	=	1 KB (kilobyte)
1024 KB	=	1 MB (megabyte)
1024 MB	=	1 GB (gigabyte)
1024 GB	=	1 TB (terabyte)

To give some idea of the size of kilobytes, megabytes, gigabytes and terabytes, small documents are typically up to 100 kB. Image files from digital
cameras usually run to a few megabytes each as do MP3 sounds files. A CD
can hold up to 800 MB or around an hour of high quality music. Low resolution full length movies are around 800 MB whilst full length high definition
movies are typically around 5 - 10 GB and take up most if not all of a DVD.
Personal computers with 4 GB of RAM and 1TB of hard disk space are now
very common.

**Bytes, Kilobytes and Megabytes are units used for the amount of
data stored in a computer. State which of these units is most appropriate for the following three items of data.** [A451 Jan 2012 Q1 (3)]

A one page text document

- Kilobyte(s)

A ten minute movie clip

- Megabyte(s)

A persons surname

- Byte(s)

**A computer has a hard disk of 2 Terabytes. How much is this in
Gigabytes? You must show your working.** (2)

- Multiply by either 1024 or 1000
- ... to give either 2048 or 2000 GBytes

**Data stored in computers can be measured in bits, bytes and kilo-
bytes. State what is meant by**

a bit [A451 Specimen Paper 2012 Q2 (1)]

- A (single) binary digit/1 or 0

a byte (1)

- A group of 8 bits

A file contains 5120 bytes. Calculate the size of the file in kilobytes. You must show your working. (2)

- Divide 5120 by 1024 giving us 5 kilobytes

4.2 NUMBER

Computers are machines, pure and simple. They can do nothing without instructions, but the instructions have to be extremely explicit. Instructions are written in languages that humans can understand, but they need to be translated into instructions that the machine can understand. Machine level instructions are made up of only two symbols, 0 and 1 which means that we need to do a little bit of maths.

Let's start with counting. We use symbols for counting and it's a surprising fact that in normal every day use, we only use ten different symbols. These are 0, 1, 2, 3, 4, 5, 6, 7, 8, 9. When we count, we start with the first symbol 0, (computer scientists always start with 0, not 1). then 1, then 2 and so on up to 9. At this point we run out of symbols, so we simply re-use them, this time putting a 1 followed by a 0 to make the number 10, which in English is called 'ten'. We then count up through the numbers 0 – 9 only this time putting a 1 in front to get the numbers $11, 12, 13, 14, 15, 16, 17, 18, 19$. There are no more symbols after 9 so we put a 2 in front and go through the sequence again, getting the numbers 20 – 29. We continue until we reach 99 at which point we simply place a 1 in front to get 100, which we call 'one hundred' and start from the beginning again. In this way we can write down any number at all.

For example, let's consider the number 5,132,407.

In our number system although we're restricted to only ten different symbols they mean different things depending on where they are. For example, counting from the right, the 7 is in the first position and so simply means seven lots of one, i.e. seven. The next symbol is a zero which in the ten position means that there are no tens. The next symbol, 4 means four hundreds, the 2 means 2 thousands, the 3 means three tens of thousands, the 1 means one hundred thousands and the final symbol, 5 is in the million position so 5,132,407 translated into words simply means 5 million, one hundred and thirty two thousand, four hundred and seven.

How do we count if we've only got two symbols.

Well, let's do it in the same way that we count in tens. We start with 0, then 1, then we repeat ourselves this time with a 1 in front to give us 10 followed by 11. To continue lets put a 1 in front and repeat giving us 100, 101, 110 and 111. These are the first eight numbers in binary and they correspond to the first eight numbers (0 – 7) in decimal (sometimes you'll see decimal called denary - it means the same thing). To get the next eight numbers we simply put a 1 in front of these and we'd get 1000, 1001, 1010, 1011, 1100, 1101, 1110 and 1111. These correspond to decimal (denary) numbers 8 – 15. Let's put this in the form of a table.

Binary	Decimal	Binary	Decimal
0000	0	1000	8
0001	1	1001	9
0010	2	1010	10
0011	3	1011	11
0100	4	1100	12
0101	5	1101	13
0110	6	1110	14
0111	7	1111	15

Let's see how a denary number such as 5,132,047 can be placed into columns of powers of ten.

You should be familiar with using exponents so that $1,000,000 = 10^6, 100,000 = 10^5, 10,000 = 10^4, 1,000 = 10^3, 100 = 10^2, 10 = 10^1$ and $1 = 10^0$. (anything to the power of 0 is 1). With this in mind, we could write 5,132,047 as

10^6	10^5	10^4	10^3	10^2	10^1	10^0
5	1	3	2	4	0	7

In exactly the same way, binary numbers can be placed in columns of powers of 2. 2^0 is 1 (because anything which has a power of 0 is 1). 2^1 is simply 2, $2^2 = 2 \times 2 = 4$, $2^3 = 2 \times 2 \times 2 = 8$ and so on up to $2^7 = 2 \times 2 \times 2 \times 2 \times 2 \times 2 \times 2 = 128$.

Let's consider the binary number 11001011 which we can express in powers of 2 in table form as shown below.

2^7	2^6	2^5	2^4	2^3	2^2	2^1	2^0
1	1	0	0	1	0	1	1

11001011 means $1 \times 2^7 + 1 \times 2^6 + 1 \times 2^3 + 1 \times 2^1 + 1 \times 2^0$ (the other powers are all 0 and anything multiplied by 0 is 0 so they don't contribute to the total). 11001011 therefore represents the denary number 128+64+8+2+1 = 203.

The binary number 00000000 has 0 in every position so means 0 in denary whilst the binary number 11111111 has a 1 in every position which means that it represents the denary number $128 + 64 + 32 + 16 + 8 + 4 + 2 + 1 = 255$. A single byte therefore can represent the denary numbers 0 – 255.

Converting Denary to Binary

We've just seen how we can convert any binary number to denary (a decimal number). How would we set about going the other way, for example converting 157 to its binary equivalent ?

Remember that an 8 bit binary number represents powers of 2 with $2^7 = 128$ being the leftmost bit. So, one way of converting a denary number to binary is to start off by asking ourselves whether our number is bigger than 128. 157 is indeed bigger than 128 so our 8 bit binary number must start with a 1.

$157 - 128 = 29$ which means that whatever the rest of our binary number is, it must represent 29. The next value of 2 is $2^6 = 64$ so we clearly don't need 64. 157 in binary must therefore start with 10. The next value of 2 is $2^5 = 32$ which again is more than 29 so we don't need 32. Our binary number therefore starts with 100. The next value of 2 is $2^4 = 16$ which is smaller than 29 so we do need one of these. Now we know that our binary number starts with 1001. If we have 16 and we needed 29 we still need $29 - 16 = 13$ more which is 8+4+1. Our binary representation of 157 is therefore 10011101.

I know that this sounds pretty convoluted, but it's harder to explain than it is to actually do. Here is one more example using a table format. In each case unknown binary bits are represent by the symbol 'x'.

Convert 237 to binary.

Decimal			Binary
237	=	128 + 109	1xxxxxxx
109	=	64 + 45	11xxxxxx
45	=	32 + 13	111xxxxx
13	=	8 + 5	11101xxx
5	=	4 + 1	11101101

This means that $237 = 1 \times 128 + 1 \times 64 + 1 \times 32 + 0 \times 16 + 1 \times 8 + 1 \times 4 + 0 \times 2 + 1 \times 1$.

Convert the denary number 106 into an 8 bit binary number. [A451 Specimen Paper 2010 Q3 (2)]

- 0110 1010 (1 mark is awarded per nibble)

Calculate the denary value of the 8-bit binary number 10010111. You must show your working. [A451 Jan 2011 Q3 (2)]

- 1001011 represents $128 + 16 + 4 + 2 + 1$
- ...which adds up to 151

Adding Binary Numbers

To understand how to add binary numbers together, let's take a quick look at adding numbers in our familiar decimal format. Let's suppose that we want to add 1,345 and 4,298. Drawn below is the usual way of doing this. (Note that **Th** is short for thousands, **H** for hundreds, **T** for tens and **U** for units, i.e. ones.

Th	H	T	U
1	3	4	5
4	2	9	8
5	6	4	3
	1	1	

So how did we do this ?

We added 5 to 8 to get 13, but we can't put 13 into the space underneath the 5 and the 8, so we split 13 into 10+3 and put the 10 into the next column. The next column is the tens column and 10 is 1 ten so we **carry** 1 across by putting it under the line.

Next we add 4 and 9 giving 13 but we must also add the 1 underneath the line to give us 14. As before we can't put 14 underneath the 9 but the 14 really means 1 hundred and 4 tens, so we put the 4 into the tens column and carry the 1 across into the hundreds column.

Next we add 3 plus 2 to give 5 and we add the 1 carried across to give us 6. This will fit into the column. There is nothing to carry into the next column.

Finally we add 1 plus 4 giving us 5 and a final answer of 5,643. Easy.

Adding binary is pretty much exactly the same, so let's add 10011100 and 01011111 together.

2^7	2^6	2^5	2^4	2^3	2^2	2^1	2^0
1	0	0	1	1	1	0	0
0	1	0	1	1	1	1	1
1	1	1	1	1	0	1	1
		1	1	1			

As with denary, we start with the rightmost or units column. (Remember 2^0 is worth 1).

We start by adding 0 to 1 to give us 1 which we can write down underneath the 1. We move on to the next column and again we need to add 0 to 1 to give us 1 again. In the third column we add 1 plus 1 to give 2. But, there are no 2s in binary. $2_D = 10_B$ which is shorthand for saying that our usual number 2 in denary is the same as binary 10. This means that we can write 0 in the third column and carry a 1 on to the fourth column.

When we add the fourth column together we get $1 + 1 + 1 = 3$ but $3_D = 11_B$ so we write 1 and carry 1 into the next (fifth) column. Here we're adding $0 + 0 + 1 = 1$ so we simply write 1 down. Finally, columns six and seven are simply adding 0 to 1 to give 1. This gives us a final binary number of 11111011.

To make sure that we've done everything correctly, it's sensible to check our answer by converting each binary to denary, adding them together and then checking that the resulting denary number is the same as our final binary number.

10011100	=	$1 \times 128 + 1 \times 16 + 1 \times 8 + 1 \times 4$	=	156
01011111	=	$1 \times 64 + 1 \times 16 + 1 \times 8 + 1 \times 4 + 1 \times 2 + 1$	=	95
11111011	=	$1 \times 128 + 1 \times 64 + 1 \times 32 + 1 \times 16 + 1 \times 8 + 1 \times 2 + 1$	=	251

$156 + 95 = 251$ so we're correct.

Some of you might have noticed that since our number has 1s in every position except the third column which represents 4 and since $11111111 = 255$, our number must be $255 - 4 = 251$.

Overflow errors

As in the following question the examiner may well ask you to add two binary numbers together and explain the result. Each binary number can range from

0 – 255 which means that when you add them together the result can range
from 0 – 510. But, the largest number that you can hold in a single byte is
255. This means that if when added together, two numbers give you a result
larger than 256, you're going to have to carry a 1 from the leftmost bit but
to where ? The answer is, to the next column which represents $2^8 = 256$.
But this is a ninth bit which currently you can't use. This is what we call
overflow. Two binary numbers that when added together give a result above
255 causes an overflow.

**Add the following two 8-bit binary numbers and explain the result.
You must show your working.** [A451 Jan 2011 Q3 (3)]

	1	0	0	1	0	1	1	1
+	1	1	0	1	1	0	0	0

Answer:

	1	0	0	1	0	1	1	1
+	1	1	0	1	1	0	0	0
1	0	1	1	0	1	1	1	1
1			1					

Marks were awarded as follows

- First nibble is correct with carries shown
- Second nibble is correct
- There is an overflow
- ... because the result > 255 and cannot be represented in 8-bits

Converting denary and binary to Hex

Following on from denary and binary it's time to look at hexadecimal numbers or hex for short. In simple terms whereas denary (our decimal system, also called base 10) uses the symbols 0 – 9 and binary (base 2) uses two symbols 0 and 1, hexadecimal is base 16 and needs 16 symbols. We use 0 – 9 and add a further 6 symbols. We could make up anything we like for these six but by convention we simply use the first six letters of the alphabet. These are usually written in capital letters and are simply the letters A – F.

So, why use Hexadecimal (Hex for short) numbers? Quite simply because it's easier to write hex numbers than it is to write binary numbers. So, the obvious next question is 'what has hex got to do with binary?'. Well, an

8 bit binary number such as 01010011 is made up of two nibbles, 0101 and 0011, where 0101 is the upper nibble and 0011 the lower. If you refer back to the table earlier on page 62, you'll see that a nibble which ranges from 0000 to 1111 holds denary numbers between 0 and 15. Hexadecimal numbers correspond to the numbers 0 – 15 which means that there is a one to one correspondence between the nibbles 0000 – 1111 and hex numbers.

Consequently, we could add another column to our table giving us

Binary	Decimal	Hex	Binary	Decimal	Hex
0000	0	0	1000	8	8
0001	1	1	1001	9	9
0010	2	2	1010	10	A
0011	3	3	1011	11	B
0100	4	4	1100	12	C
0101	5	5	1101	13	D
0110	6	6	1110	14	E
0111	7	7	1111	15	F

With this in mind, the binary number 01010011 can be written as two nibbles 0101 0011 each of which could be written as a single hex number, giving us in this case the hex number 53.

When binary numbers are written it's usually pretty obvious that they are binary numbers unless we have written down only two or three bits, for example, 10 or 101 which could quite easily be mistaken for the decimal numbers ten and one hundred and one. Hex numbers are unfortunately far less obvious. For example is 93 the decimal number ninety three or the hexadecimal number equivalent to the binary number 10010011?

To avoid any ambiguity, it's usually a very good idea to either write the word 'hex' or a letter 'H' (usually but not necessarily capitalised) next to the number such as 53H.

To convert denary to hex we could simply convert denary to binary and then write out the two nibbles as two hex numbers, but there is a much quicker way **if** you know your sixteen times table.

$$
\begin{aligned}
1 \times 16 &= 16 \\
2 \times 16 &= 32 \\
3 \times 16 &= 48 \\
4 \times 16 &= 64 \\
5 \times 16 &= 80 \\
6 \times 16 &= 96 \\
7 \times 16 &= 112 \\
8 \times 16 &= 128 \\
9 \times 16 &= 144 \\
A \times 16 &= 160 \\
B \times 16 &= 176 \\
C \times 16 &= 192 \\
D \times 16 &= 208 \\
E \times 16 &= 224 \\
F \times 16 &= 240
\end{aligned}
$$

Let's suppose we're asked what is the hexadecimal equivalent of the denary number 157.

If we look at our times table we can see that the largest number less than 157 is 144 which is 9×16, so our hex number will start with 9. $157 - 144 = 13 = D$ so our second hex number is D giving us 9D hex because $157 = 9 \times 16 + 13$. What about the denary number 223? The largest number from our table less than 223 is 208 which is $D \times 16$ so our hex number starts with D. $223 - 208 = 15 = F$ so our second hex number is F giving us the hex number DF.

This is a very quick way of converting denary to hex, and you might notice also a very quick way of converting denary to binary. Because, if for example, the denary number $157 = 9D$ hex and 9D hex $= 10011101$ then $157 = 1001$ 1101.

Take the decimal number 117. $117 = 7 \times 16 + 5$ so $117 = 75H = 0111\ 0101$. Quick isn't it. But **only if** you know **both** your sixteen times table **and** the binary to hex table on page 67.

Why does this work? Well, hexadecimal is base 16 which means that just as we write denary numbers as powers of 10 and binary numbers as powers of 2, hexadecimal numbers are powers of 16. This means that a hexadecimal number such as $2AB5 = 2 \times 16^3 + 10 \times 16^2 + 11 \times 16^1 + 5 = 10,933$ in denary.

Convert the hexadecimal number 6A to denary. You must show your working. [A451 Jun 2011 Q6 (2)]

- $6A = 6 * 16 + 10$
- i.e. $96 + 10 = 106$

Convert the denary number 106 into Hexadecimal. [A451 Specimen Paper 2010 Q3 (2)]

- 6A (1 mark is awarded per digit)

Convert the hexadecimal number 6A to binary. [A451 Jun 2011 Q6 (2)]

- 0110 1010 (a mark for each nibble)

Convert the binary number 00111101 to hexadecimal. (2)

- 3D (a mark for each digit)

Why use Hex?

So, why use Hex? I suppose that the simplest answer is that it is much easier to read and write in hex than it is to read and write binary, and hex and binary have a one to one relationship. One nibble (i.e. four bits) of binary is exactly equivalent to a single hex digit as the table on page 67 shows.

Some computer scientists, especially those writing software directly onto hardware, such as some game developers, will often have to work in binary and it is much easier to remember hex numbers such as C3 than their binary equivalent 11000011.

Explain why hexadecimal numbers are often used to represent binary numbers. [A451 Jun 2011 Q6 (2)]

- Hex numbers are shorter and more memorable than equivalent binary numbers
- ... and can easily be converted to and from binary
- ... as each hex digit corresponds to 4 binary digits

4.3 CHARACTER

Binary Codes

One byte is capable of storing 256 different numbers ranging from 00000000
– 11111111 or in denary 0 – 255. Early on in the development of computer
science, scientists realised that code instructions could be defined in terms
of particular binary patterns and that characters such as the letter 'A' could
also be associated with particular binary patterns. In which case, a binary
pattern such as 01000001 could when decoded represent the instruction 'add
the contents of the B register to the A register, leaving the result in the A
register', or it could simply mean the letter 'A'. The obvious question is well,
which is it? Is 01000001 an instruction or does it represent the character 'A'?

The answer is that it can be both, it all depends on context. If the pattern
01000001 is found inside a piece of code then it means 'add the contents of
the B register to the A register, leaving the result in the A register', whereas
if it is found inside a data area it means the letter 'A'. Binary patterns can
be code or data depending on context. The important thing to remember is
that any particular binary bit pattern can potentially represent an instruction or a character depending on context.

Character Sets

Let's look at how we might associate binary numbers with characters. One
byte gives us 256 different numbers to play with. If we want to be able
to write English words we need 26 numbers for the upper case letters and
another 26 for the lowercase letters. We need another 10 for the numbers
0 – 9 and some more for punctuation marks and arithmetic symbols such as
'!@£$%&+-=' and so on. This will bring us to around 100 in total which
suggests that we can associate each character with a particular byte and still
have over half the available numbers left over.

Various groups of computer scientists went through this very process and
after much discussion agreed on a standard way of associating 8 bit binary
patterns with characters. One group working for IBM agreed on a particular way, this table of associations is called EBCDIC. Another group came
up with what is called the **American Standard Code for Information
Interchange** or **ASCII** for short. This has a different table of associations.
The EBCDIC table isn't used a great deal these days, but the ASCII table
is used world wide and part of it is shown below.

ASCII

Dec	Hex	ASCII	Dec	Hex	ASCII	Dec	Hex	ASCII
032	20	␣	048	30	0	064	40	@
033	21	!	049	31	1	065	41	A
034	22	"	050	32	2	066	42	B
035	23	#	051	33	3	067	43	C
036	24	$	052	34	4	068	44	D
037	25	%	053	35	5	069	45	E
038	26	&	054	36	6	070	46	F
039	27	'	055	37	7	071	47	G
040	28	(	056	38	8	072	48	H
041	29	)	057	39	9	073	49	I
042	2A	*	058	3A	:	074	4A	J
043	2B	+	059	3B	;	075	4B	K
044	2C	,	060	3C	¡	076	4C	L
045	2D	-	061	3D	=	077	4D	M
046	2E	.	062	3E	¿	078	4E	N
047	2F	/	063	3F	?	079	4F	O

The three columns represent the denary number, its hexadecimal equivalent and the character these numbers represent. For example, the letter 'A' is agreed by computer scientists world wide to be associated with the denary number 65, which is equivalent to the hex number 41 and therefore the binary number 01000001. The letter 'B' is 66 denary which is 42 hex and equivalent to the binary number 01000010.

UNICODE

ASCII is fine for representing languages where the character set is alphabetic such as English. Most of the European languages and some Asian languages form a family of several hundred languages under the heading of Indo-European. All of these use an alphabetic system that can be encoded in 8 bits, but there are a number of languages in the world, Chinese and Japanese foremost amongst them that are composed of many thousands of different characters and cannot be encoded in 8 bits. Computer scientists therefore developed UNICODE, an encoding system that uses up to 32 bits (in two 16 bit units) to encode any character from any character set.

All modern computer systems understand UNICODE. The unicode encoding UTF-8 is equivalent to ASCII which means that all modern computer systems also understand ASCII.

State what is meant by the character set of a computer. [A451 Jan 2011 Q10 (1)]

- All the characters which are recognised can be represented by the computer system

Explain how ASCII is used to represent text in a computer system. [A451 Jan 2011 Q10 (3)]

- Each character is given a numeric code
- . . . including symbols, digits, upper and lower case
- This code is then stored in binary
- Each character takes 1 byte
- Text is stored as a series of bytes (1 per character)
- Some codes are reserved for control characters (e.g. TAB, Carriage Return)

Unicode is also used to represent text in a computer system. Explain the difference between the character sets of Unicode and ASCII. (2)

- Unicode has a much larger character set
- . . . and can represent many more characters and indeed characters from all alphabets
- Because unicode uses 16 bits
- . . . and ASCII uses fewer (7/8 bits)

4.4 IMAGES

Images are everywhere. What would the web be without images. The old adage says that a picture is worth a thousand words. Imagine trying to describe an elephant without using a photograph of one, or a computer system to someone who had never seen one. Images enhance understanding.

Not so very long ago, pictures were taken with cameras that opened and closed shutters that allowed light in onto a strip of photographic emulsion 'film'. The cartridge containing the film was removed from the camera, the film extracted in a 'dark room' and then immersed in a bath of chemicals to 'fix' the image onto the film. Projectors were then used to shine the image on the film onto special photographic paper. The paper was then immersed in a bath of the right combination of chemicals. All of this had to take place in a room lit only by red light.

Since then, there has been a digital revolution, and the overwhelming majority of cameras today use **Charge Coupled Devices (CCDs)** to convert light into binary data that can be stored on some form of (usually) magnetic media.

The majority of images stored on computer systems are stored in the form of **bitmaps**. These are files where the pattern of bits represent pixel information. Picture elements, or **pixels** for short are single dots on the screen of your digital TV or computer monitor. If you look ever so closely at the screen, you may see that the screen is made up of distinct dots and if you are using a very old screen you might even notice that each dot is in fact made up of three overlapping dots, one representing each of what are called the three **primary colours** - red, green and blue. They are called primary, because the combination of differing intensities of each of red, green and blue will give us the astonishing range of colours that we see on screen. You may know that if you use a prism it is possible to 'split' light into the range of colours that we see in the rainbow. In a somewhat similar fashion, but done digitally, digital cameras capture light and record the intensity of its red, green and blue components.

In most colour formats, each colour is represented by one byte and since one byte can hold 256 different numbers in the range 0−255, each colour can have an intensity ranging from 0 which means no colour, to 255 which means full colour. With three colours to play with we have $256 \times 256 \times 256 = 16,777,216$ different colours, ranging from black (all colours set to zero) to white (all colours set to maximum, i.e. 255).

The **colour depth** of an image refers to the number of bits used to store the colour of a single pixel in an image. For example, if we use one one byte per colour to store each of the red, green and blue components of a pixel, the colour depth would be 24. The **resolution** of an image is the term used to describe the size of an image in pixels. For example, a small image on a web page might have a resolution of 200×120 which indicates that the image is 200 pixels wide by 120 pixels high.

Peter takes a high resolution picture with a digital camera. The picture is stored in a bitmap file. Describe how a picture is stored in a bitmap file. [A451 Specimen Paper 2010 Q4 (3)]

- The picture is split into dots/pixel

- Each pixel is given a binary code (which says what colour it is)
- The bitmap file contains the list of pixels
- ... and header/meta information on how to display them (e.g. height and width, resolution, colour depth)

Image Formats

There are a variety of different pixel formats in current use today. Each format saves pixel information in its own way. Some formats specify that each pixel is made up of the three primary colours and that each colour takes up one byte. Consequently, in this format, a single pixel is stored as three bytes. Others, GIF for example, use a single byte to store colour information, with the value of the byte representing an index into a palette of 256 colours, each of which is defined in RGB (red/green/blue) format of one byte per colour. This means that the palette takes up $256 \times 3 = 768$ bytes. Still others store only black and white information, in which case whether a pixel is black or white can be stored as individual bits with 0 representing a black pixel and 1 representing white.

Information about data is called **metadata**. When pixel information is saved in a file, metadata about such things as image resolution, colour depth and whether and what type of compression algorithm is being used is also stored. Some formats such as TIFF store raw data about every pixel whilst others such as JPG result in smaller files at the expense of data that is considered unnecessary.

To give an idea of what these different formats mean in terms of size, let's consider three different image formats, each of which encodes an image which has a resolution of 1200 pixels wide, by 600 pixels high. An image which is 1200 pixels wide by 600 pixels high has a total of $1200 \times 600 = 720,000$ pixels. The table that follows shows how much storage each of these images will take when stored in each particular format.

Format	Calculation	Size (in bytes)
Black and white, 1 bit per pixel	$720,000/8$	90,000
Colour, 1 byte per pixel + pallette	$720,000 + 256 \times 3$	720,768
Colour, 3 bytes per pixel	$720,000 \times 3$	2,160,000

As you can see from the this example, the size of files of the same resolution, in this case 1200×600 varies from $90,000$ to $2,160,000$ bytes depending on how many colours we want in our image. Note that laser printers print at a resolution of 600 dots per inch, so assuming each dot represents a pixel, the resulting printed image would be only 2 inches (5 cm) wide by 1 inch (2.5

cm) high.

Question : How large would a full colour image file be if it were the size of an A4 sheet of page printed out at a typical laser resolution of 600 dots per inch? Think about this for some time before reading on.

Answer : An A4 sheet of paper is roughly 11 inches by 9 inches, i.e. roughly 100 square inches and each square inch is made up of $600 \times 600 = 360,000$ dots. Since each dot is equivalent to a pixel this means $360,000$ pixels per inch.

Each pixel is made up of three colours, red, green and blue and each colour needs one byte. So, total size is $100 \times 360,000 \times 3 = 108,000,000$ bytes or a little over 100 MBytes.

With this sort of space requirement, it's no surprise that computer scientists have spent quite some time on looking at ways of reducing the size of these images, but keeping the same resolution. Reducing the size of a file is called **compressing** it and there are a number of ways we might tackle this depending on whether we're happy to lose information in doing so.

Lossless compression algorithms aim to reduce the size of the file **without** losing information. There are various ways that they might do this. For example, let's suppose that we have a full colour image on a white background. Line after line of pixels will be white, so instead of saving each pixel as three bytes, why not simply save the number of bytes that are white instead. If the image is 1200×600 the three top rows might each consist of only white pixels, i.e. $1200 \times 3 = 3,600$ white pixels. If we stored each of these in three bytes, we'd need $3,600 \times 3 = 10,800$ bytes. If on the other hand, we simply stored the number 10,800 followed by three bytes of 255 this would only need 5 bytes of storage (2 bytes for the number 10,800 and 3 for the colour information) instead of $10,800$. This is a huge saving.

With clever techniques like this it is possible to reduce a file quite considerably without losing any information.

If however we are prepared to lose information, there are all sorts of mathematical algorithms that have been designed to reduce the file size very considerably. Size reductions of 10:1 are common, and some complex fractal algorithms are able to reduce the size of image files by over 100:1. These are enormous savings and very important if you're waiting for an image file to download off the Internet.

The following graphic file formats are amongst the most common file formats found in use today.

TIFF

Tagged Image Format Files (TIFF) files store information pretty much exactly as is. This means that if for example, your camera is a 10 megapixel camera, each image it captures is made up of 10 million picture elements. Since each pixel consists of three bytes, this gives us a total required storage of roughly 30 MBytes. This is quite a lot, and a typical 4 GByte micro disk will store around 130 images.

JPEG

Files that conform to the format laid down by the Joint Photographic Expert Group (JPEG) do not store all of the information that the camera records. Using some very sophisticated algorithms, the image data is analysed, some of it is thrown away and an image file saved that is very much smaller than would be saved in TIFF format. JPEG files are typically only 10% of the size of the corresponding TIFF file. This means that a 4 GByte micro disk will store closer to 1,300 images rather than the 130 or so in TIFF format. Admittedly, the saved image file will be of slightly poorer quality than the TIFF file, but this is unnoticeable except when scaled up quite large.

GIF

Graphics Interchange Format (GIF) files are an old file format but you still see them used today on the web. They use only a single byte per pixel which means that they are limited to a maximum of 256 colours. However, each file includes within it a **palette** of colours chosen from the full range of red, green and blue combinations that are used in JPEG and TIFF. Each pixel is an index into the colour palette. With this limitation, GIF files are clearly not terribly good for recording photographs but for line art and images which only require a small number of colours they are ideal. Since they only use one byte per pixel they are usually small and are very effective on web pages especially as they can record simple animations.

PNG

Finally we should mention Portable Network Graphics (PNG) files. They were created in response to Unisys and Compuserve who owned patents on the GIF format suddenly demanding royalties from those companies and individuals who used GIF files. PNG files are an attempt to provide an effective replacement to GIF, but which also incorporate the advantages of small size and animations without any associated legal problems.

You will come across all of these file formats in your course; each has its advantages and disadvantages. TIFF files retain all image information but at the cost of large file size. JPEG files are very much smaller but they achieve this at the cost of loss of information. GIF files are restricted to 256 colour or greyscale images but have the advantage of being to able to show animations. PNG files are smaller than GIF in 256 colour mode and compete effectively with JPEG in full colour mode. They lose information like JPEG but like GIF can also deliver animations.

Peter takes a picture of himself and his friends to put on a social networking site. The picture is converted into pixels and stored as a bitmap file. Tick one box in each row to show whether or not each of the following items must be included in the bitmap file. [A451 Jan 2012 Q5 (5)]

	Must be included	Need not be included
The names of the people in the picture		
The width of the picture in pixels		
The number of bits used for each pixel		
The number of people in the picture		
The colour of each pixel		

Answer

	Must be included	Need not be included
The names of the people in the picture		✓
The width of the picture in pixels	✓	
The number of bits used for each pixel	✓	
The number of people in the picture		✓
The colour of each pixel	✓	

Peter takes a picture of himself and his friends to put on a social networking site. The picture is converted into pixels and stored as a bitmap file. What is meant by the resolution of the picture? [A451 Jan 2012 Q5 (1)]

- The concentration of pixels
- The width and height of the picture in pixels

How does the resolution affect the size of the bitmap file? (2)

- The higher the resolution, more pixels are required for the picture
- ... which will increase the size of the bitmap file
- Alternatively, lower resolution implies fewer pixels
- ... and a smaller size

Peter wants to send a high resolution digital picture as an email attachment. State two methods for reducing the size of the picture file so that it is suitable for sending as an email. [A451 Specimen Paper 2010 Q4 (2)]

- Resize the image/picture to reduce the number of pixels
- Reduce the colour depth to reduce the number of bits needed to store each pixel
- Compress the file

4.5 SOUND

Sound is another important area that has been very effectively digitised over recent years. Some thirty years ago a budding young musician would have owned a bulky second or third hand multi-track reel to reel machine that used cassette tape to record the guitars, drums and keyboard that made up the music. Microphones would pick up the sound from the instruments and each would be saved to a separate track. The tracks would be mixed in a mixing desk and a recording of the whole ensemble produced.

These machines have been replaced today with computer systems running software applications that can synthesise its own sounds and/or import data from microphones listening to individual instruments. Once in the computer, each instrument can be modified at will and the sound filtered, enhanced and improved in all sorts of interesting ways.

But, what is sound?

According to one source, Sound is *"vibrations transmitted through an elastic solid or a liquid or gas, with frequencies in the approximate range of 20 to 20,000 hertz, capable of being detected by human organs of hearing"*[1]. So, sound is set of vibrations, i.e. a wave of some sort and it's clear from the definition that sound can be transmitted in air, in water and in solids. Hearing sounds in air is something that we're all familiar with. Some of us will have

---

[1]The American Heritage Dictionary of the English Language

experienced hearing underwater - talking underwater is tricky, but hearing is ok, though somewhat strange. Sound waves are also transmitted through solids which is why in some Western cowboy films you see the characters with their ears pressed to the railway lines listening for the sound of an approaching train.

For those who are interested, in dry air at 20°C the speed of sound is 343.2 ms^{-1}. In fresh water at 25°C, sounds travels at 1,497 ms^{-1} and in steel the speed of sound is around 6,000 ms^{-1}.

Waves are defined by three things, their amplitude, their wavelength and their frequency. Amplitude refers to the maximum height of the wave above it's mean value and for us, this means how loud it is. The greater the amplitude, the more energy it has and the louder it sounds. Wavelength refers to the distance between subsequent peaks or troughs. Frequency refers to how many peaks (or troughs) pass per second (strictly speaking, per time interval, but we'll stick to seconds). We hear frequency in terms of pitch, as the frequency of sound increases, so does its pitch. The higher the frequency, the higher the pitch. Purely for interest (you're certainly not going to be examined on this) the table below[2] gives an idea of the range of common animals (including us).

Species	Range (Hz)	Species	Range (Hz)
tuna	50 − 1,100	hedgehog	250 − 45,000
goldfish	20 − 3,000	dog	67 − 45,000
chicken	125 − 2,000	guinea pig	54 − 50,000
owl	200 − 12,000	gerbil	100 − 60,000
elephant	16 − 12,000	cat	45 − 64,000
human	20 − 23,000	rat	200 − 76,000
sheep	100 − 30,000	mouse	1,000 − 91,000
horse	55 − 33,500	bat	2,000 − 110,000
cow	23 − 35,000	beluga whale	1,000 − 123,000
rabbit	360 − 42,000	porpoise	75 − 150,000

Sampling

A wave represents an analogue signal, meaning that it if you look at the waveform and measure the height of the wave at any arbitrary point, you'll get some value. It doesn't have to be some whole number such as 1 or 2 or 3, but could be 1.3452 (to 4 d.p.), 0.567234 (to 6 d.p.), or indeed anything.

---

[2]Louisiana State University, deafness research

At some point, a wave that rises from 0 to 1 takes on every possible value between these two numbers. But there are an infinite number of numbers between 0 and 1. Computers work in binary, i.e. zeros and ones. They can't handle infinite values which means that somehow, the wave needs to be converted from an analogue signal to a digital signal.

This job is done by an **analogue-to-digital** or **A-D converter**. This device samples (measures the height of) the waveform at discrete intervals, perhaps 44,100 times per second if you're recording sound of CD quality, more frequently if you're aiming at professional quality. A-D converters are also defined in terms of their resolution, i.e. how accurately they can represent the waveform that they sample. An 8-bit A-D converter has a resolution of 8 bits, i.e. it can 'see' only 256 different values in the waveform. If a waveform ranges from say 0 to 16,000, an 8 bit A-D converter would divide the range into 256 discrete values with each bit recording a change of 62.5, This means that so that if the converter read a value from the waveform in the range $0-62.5$, it would record a 0000 0000, if between $62.5-126$ it would record 0000 0001 and so on, recording 1111 1111 for the range $15937.5-16000$.

An A-D converter aiming at CD quality sound will sample the waveform using a resolution of 16 bits giving 2^{16}, i.e. 65,536 different discrete levels. Looking at the same waveform, a 16-bit A-D converter would record 00000000 00000000 for heights of the waveform in the range $0-0.244140625$, 00000000 00000001 for the range $0.2551506251-0.48828125$ and so on up to 11111111 11111111 for the range $15999.75586-16000$.

Clearly a 16 bit A-D will give us a much better, and to our ears more accurate approximation to the actual waveform than an 8-bit A-D converter.

Sampling at CD quality requires considerable storage. Let's suppose that we wanted to sample sound lasting one minute at full CD quality. We'd use a 16-bit A-D converter sampling at 44.1 KHz (i.e. 44,100). This means storing 16 bits, i.e. 2 bytes, 44,100 times per second. This is 88,200 bytes per second or $60 \times 88200 = 5292000$ bytes, or roughly 6 MBytes for each minute of sound. If we were sampling in stereo, we'd need to double this requiring 12 MBytes of storage per minute of sound.

Clearly the more samples you take per second and the more bits you have available to your analog to digital converter, the better will be your sound quality, though at the expense of a larger file. Music CDs typically can typically hold up to 800MB of data and given that at stereo CD quality we need 12 MBytes per minute, a music CD will store at most around 70 minutes of songs.

As with graphics files, it is perfectly possible to compress sound files and clever algorithms have been designed to save sound files in both lossless and lossy formats. Examples of lossless compression formats include FLAC (Free Lossless Audio Codec) and ALAC (Apple Lossless Audio Codec) whilst the most common example of lossy sound compression is the ubiquitous MP3 (MPEG-2 Audio Layer III) file format. MP3 files can reduce a 30MB song to around 3MB which means that it is possible to store 10 times the number of songs in MP3 format compared to uncompressed CD quality format. In order to achieve such impressive compression ratios, an MP3 file will throw away a great deal of what is considered to be unnecessary information. However, since most MP3 files are played through rather poor quality headphones and speakers the reduction in quality that such compression produces is not normally noticeable.

An artist is recording sound using a computer. The graph below represents the pressure wave of the sound being recorded.

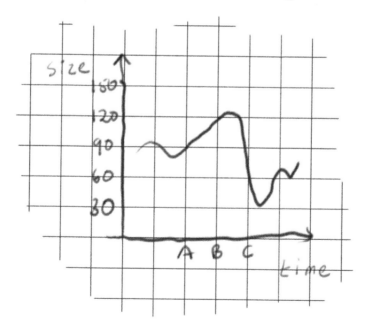

At point A on the graph, the size of the sound wave is 90. This is stored digitally using the binary value of 0101 1010 (or 5A in Hex).

Complete the table below to show how points B and C are stored:
[A451 Specimen Paper 2012 Q9 (6)]

	Point A	Point B	Point C
Size	90		
Binary Value	0101 1010		
Hex Value	5A		

Answer:

	Point A	Point B	Point C
Size	90	120	60
Binary Value	0101 1010	0111 1000	0011 1100
Hex Value	5A	78	3C

Explain how sampling intervals and compression can affect the size of a sound file and the quality of its playback. The quality of written communication will be assessed in your answer to this question.
[A451 Specimen Paper 2012 Q9 (8)]

The examiners expected that the following points would be made.

- Sampling Rate
  - how close together the samples are taken
  - the closer together, the more numbers need to be stored (and therefore larger file)
  - but the sound that is created is closer to the original analogue
  - mention of variable bit rates
- Compression
  - uses algorithms to make the file smaller (e.g. for transmitting over Internet)
  - and then recreated to be played
  - can be lossy (e.g. MP3) and the recreated file is of poorer quality
  - or lossless (e.g. FLAC) and the recreated file is exactly the same as it was before compression

4.6 THE MICROPROCESSOR INSTRUCTION SET

As we discussed briefly back on page 9, a microprocessor is a machine, a machine made out of silicon rather than metal, but a machine nevertheless.

Modern microprocessors have over 500 million transistors. These transistors are grouped into patterns that make up logic gates, and logic gates are grouped to provide useful functions. These functions make up the instruction set of the microprocessor.

It is important that you understand a little of what a microprocessor actually is in addition to what it does.

To start with, all microprocessors have a small number of **registers**. There are three essential registers that are found on any microprocessor. These are the **Accumulator**, the **Program Counter (PC)** and the **flags** register.

Think of an accumulator as a small scratch pad on which you can write a single number. You can replace the number with another, you can add or subtract a number to the number in the accumulator and on each occasion the answer is left in the accumulator.

You can copy a number from RAM into the accumulator, write a number from the accumulator to RAM and do a small number of logical operations. These usually include ANDing a number with the number in the accumulator, ORing it, XORing and negating it, again leaving the answer in the accumulator.

The instructions that the microprocessor runs are always stored in RAM (or when starting up, in ROM). The program counter **always** holds the address of the next instruction that is going to be fetched into the CPU prior to decoding and execution. It controls the flow of instructions into the CPU. After every fetch, the program counter is incremented to point to the next instruction to be fetched. Usually, this is simply the next instruction in RAM. However, in addition to the arithmetic and logical instructions, there are invariably a small set of instructions which allow the microprocessor to make a decision based on the value of the number in the accumulator. For example, there is usually an instruction such as `JMPZ address`, meaning jump if zero to `address`, where `address` is the address in RAM of the next instruction to be fetched if the contents of the accumulator have, as a result of the previous instruction been set to zero.

The microprocessor will know if the contents of the accumulator are zero because whenever an instruction completes its execution the flags register is updated to reflect any changes. Depending on whether the microprocessor is an 8-bit, 16-bit, 32-bit or 64-bit microprocessor, the flags register will be 8, 16, 32 or 64 bits wide. Each bit represents a single **state**. For example one bit (the **zero flag**) will be set (i.e. 1) if the accumulator is currently holding a zero and 0 if it is not. Another bit in the **flags** flags register indicates whether the previous calculation resulted in a number too large to fit int the accumulator. This condition would arise for example, if you tried to add the two bytes 1100 1100 and 1110 0011 together. The result is (1) 1010 1111. Here both numbers were large enough so that when we added them together they exceeded the capacity of one byte. In this instance the **carry flag**, or depending on whether the calculation is signed, the **overflow flag** would be set.

Bit Patterns

Microprocessors understand only binary. Similarly the RAM holds only binary numbers. In fact, as you now know, all data and code are encoded as a group of zeros and ones. These groups invariably are multiples of 8 bits or one byte in size. Each instruction in the instruction set of a microprocessor is encoded as a group of binary digits. In an 8 bit computer, each instruction is typically 8 bits, or one byte wide. For example the bit pattern 0110 0011 might when decoded by the microprocessor mean `Add one to the accumulator`. The bit pattern 1100 0010 might mean `Clear all bits in the accumulator`, thus setting it to zero. The bit pattern 0011 1100 might very well mean `Copy the contents of the address that you find in the next location in RAM into the accumulator`. In this case the bit pattern 0011 1100 might be followed by 0010 1010 and if address 0010 1010 held the binary number 0000 0101 then the full instruction would result in the number 0000 0101, i.e. 5 being copied into the accumulator.

The following table (included purely to help you understand what really happens in a typical microprocessor - **you will not be examined on this**) is a snapshot of selected parts of the instruction set of the 8080 microprocessor, an early Intel processor used in the first IBM PC. The 8080 was an 16 bit computer with six registers (B, C, D, E, H, L) in addition to the accumulator A. Note that the machine code instruction is written in hex. Hex is easily converted to binary using the table on page 67. The first machine instruction 7F is equivalent to 0111 1111 in binary. In the last five instructions illustrated, **address** would be the address in RAM where the program counter would need to get its next instruction from if the specified condition was met.

Mnemonic	Machine Code	Operation
MOV A,A	7F	A ← A
MOV A,B	78	A ← B
MOV A,C	79	A ← C
MOV A,D	7A	A ← D
MOV A,E	7B	A ← E
MOV A,H	7C	A ← H
MOV A,L	7D	A ← L
MOV B,A	47	B ← A
MOV B,B	40	B ← B
ADD A	87	A ← A + A
ADD B	80	A ← A + B
XRA A	AF	A ← A XOR A
XRA B	A8	A ← A XOR B
JMP address	C3 address	PC ← address
JNZ address	C2 address	If NZ, PC ← address
JZ address	CA address	If Z, PC ← address
JNC address	D2 address	If NC, PC ← address
JC address	DA address	If C, PC ← address

Instructions or Data

If everything in RAM is held in binary, what is there to distinguish between instructions and data that the instructions are operating on? The answer is that there is no way of distinguishing them simply by looking. For example as you may recall from the section on character sets on page 70, the capital letter G has ASCII code 71 in denary, 47 in hex. If you look back at the instructions set above, you'll see that if 47 is loaded into the 8080 microprocessor, the microprocessor will decode it and will respond by copying the contents of the B register into the A register. 47 hex can either mean G or it can mean copy the contents of the B register into the accumulator.

So how do we distinguish between them? The answer is that it all depends on context. When the programmer writes her code she clearly distinguishes between the program code and the data. When the compiler converts the program to binary code it will maintain the distinction and when the loader loads the program into RAM, code is put into the code area and data in the data area. The microprocessor fetches instructions from the code area and data from the data area, and all being well there is never a mixup. However, there are situations where if the programmer has been careless writing his software, it is possible for the code to stray into the data area in which case the program counter might very well start picking up bit patterns from the data area which the microprocessor will then interpret as if they were code. At which point the program will almost certainly crash.

Databases

5.1 THE DATABASE CONCEPT

A Database *"is a (large) collection of data items and links between them, structured in a way that allows it to be accessed by a number of different application programs. The term is also used loosely to describe any collection of data"*[1]. So, a database is a persistent organised store of data, perhaps holding information about you such as your name, home telephone number, date of birth or last maths test mark for example. Databases store data, information of some sort, and very importantly, information that needs to be kept in such a way that it can be easily retrieved.

A television set top box contains a database of television channels and programmes. Describe what is meant by a database. [A451 Specimen Paper 2012 Q5 (2)]

- A set of data
- ...organised
- ...as a set of records
- ...in one or more files

5.2 THE DBMS

A database management system (DBMS) is software that can find data in a database, add new data and change existing data. A DBMS may provide its own simple user interface, or more commonly, communicate with external programs using a **Data Manipulation Language (DML)**. The most common of these today is **Structured Query Language (SQL)**. The description of which data items are stored together with the relationships between them are written in a **data description language (DDL)**. The DDL

---

[1] British Computer Society Glossary of Computing and ICT

defines the schema, creates tables, create attributes, defines data types, primary and foreign keys and the validation rules. Many systems today use XML and/or SQL as their DDL. The **data dictionary** is a file containing descriptions of, and other information about the structure of the data held in the database.

For those of you who are familiar with Microsoft Access this program is an excellent example of a DMBS. Using it, you can create a database and tables of records and fields of information. It has facilities to let you populate tables, records and fields with data and it allows you to set up relationships between tables. It provides a means of querying the database and it facilitates the design and construction of reports which can be created in response to queries that you set up. Finally, you can use it to create a simple user interface to carry out many of these tasks.

When you use Access to create tables, records and fields and when you use it to create primary and foreign keys to join tables together you are using its data description language (DDL). When you use it to fill in the fields with data, query it and generate reports you are using its data manipulation language (DML).

Every instruction to the DBMS such as creating and deleting databases, creating, deleting and modifying tables, records and fields, inserting and deleting data from tables and creating primary and foreign keys is written in a language understood by the DMBS. This language is generally hidden from you when you use programs such as Microsoft Access, since a much simpler 'point and click' interface is available to do these tasks. Behind the scenes however, Access uses SQL to perform these tasks. The examiners will expect you to understand a little of some of the syntax of SQL particularly in regard to making queries. We cover this a little later on page 98.

One important aspect of a DBMS is that it separates the data that is held in the database from the applications that wish to access the data. An important consequence of this is that different users can be given different views on the same data. This is very desirable. For example, imagine that we have a large company selling food products. The company has 100 employees and uses a database to hold information on each employee and each food product. For employees it stores their names, addresses, telephone numbers, salary details, national insurance numbers and position within the company. It also stores information on its suppliers, their names, addresses, products they sell and at what prices, who within the company deals with them, contact information including addresses and telephones numbers and bank details.

It also stores customer details including products sold, invoice information and so on. It stores information about the products it sells such as which suppliers each can purchased, number of sales for each product and dates. All in all a very large amount of data is stored.

For a receptionist within the company, the majority of this information is clearly irrelevant. He (or she) might need to know names, internal telephone numbers and perhaps mobile numbers for some employees but most probably should not have access to employee confidential information such as salary details and national insurance numbers. The sales manager on the other hand should be allowed to see product sales information, customer orders and how well each of the salesmen are doing. The financial director should have access to salary and national insurance information whilst the managing director should have access to whatever he or she needs in order to run the company most effectively.

The DBMS can be set up to allow this by enforcing differing levels of security dependent on the level within the company of each employee.

A grocery shop uses a database with a DBMS to keep records of its stock. Explain what is meant by a DBMS. [A451 Jun 2011 Q2 (3)]

- A Database Management System used to manage the database
- It may use SQL or some other query language which allows the database to be queried
- It provides facilities for creating tables, inserting data, viewing data and reporting
- It allows the database data structure to be independent of the program
- It allows relationships to be created between tables and maintains integrity
- It provides security features and different levels of access

5.3 FLAT FILE AND RELATIONAL DATABASES

The simplest type of database is called a **flat file database**. It consists of a single table which stores all of the data that we wish to keep. Flat files are fine for very small amounts of data, but quickly become very difficult to update whilst remaining consistent as the amount of stored data increases.

To illustrate what a flat file database looks like let's suppose that we want to keep track of our CD collection. For each CD we'd probably want to keep track of the title, the artist and possibly the label information (RCA, Sony

Music etc). A short example of such a database might be similar to the following table.

Name	Artist	Label
Safe trip home	Dido	RCA
Girl who got away	Dido	Sony Music
White flag	Dido	Aristo
Cold shoulder	Adele	XL
Home town glory	Adele	XL
Elephant	White Stripes	XL
Icky Thump	White Stripes	XL
Broken boy soldiers	White Stripes	XL

Each line in this table is called a **record**. Each record stores information about a particular CD. Each column holds a piece of information. We call each column a **field**. Our simple database is holding 8 records, one for each CD and each record consists of 3 fields holding data on the title of the CD, the artist and the label. Generally, a database could therefore be thought of as a collection of records where each record is a collection of fields.

If we wanted to keep some more information on the artists, perhaps the town where they were born, their date of birth and nationality we could create three more **fields** giving us the following table.

Name	Artist	DoB	Town	Nationality	Label
Safe trip home	Dido	25-12-71	London	English	RCA
Girl who got away	Dido	25-12-71	London	English	Sony Music
White flag	Dido	25-12-71	London	English	Aristo
Cold shoulder	Adele	5-5-1988	London	English	XL
Home town glory	Adele	5-5-1988	Londn	English	XL
Elephant	White Stripes	1997	Detroit	American	XL
Icky Thump	White Stripes	1997	Detroit	American	XL
Broken boy soldiers	White Stripes	1997	Detroit	American	XL

The first thing to notice is that we have to enter the same data more than once. In our example we have to enter Dido's date of birth three times. This isn't a good thing since we are pretty much bound to make mistakes. It would be much better if when we enter data, we only enter it only once. You might have noticed that the second entry for Adele has her home town as 'Londn' whereas it should have been 'London'. If we were searching for all CDs of artists born in London we'd miss out on 'Home town glory'.

In order to avoid this sort of data duplication we can use a **relational database** instead where each real world object which in database technology is called an **entity** has its own table. Records within each table are ordered

according to a unique **primary key** and tables are linked together using
these keys. If we reconstruct our simple flat file database by creating one
table to represent each of the real world entities, CD, artist and label, we
end up with the following three tables.

CD

CD_ID	Title	Artist_ID	Label_ID
1	Safe trip home	1	1
2	Girl who got away	1	2
3	White flag	1	3
4	Cold shoulder	2	4
5	Home town glory	2	4
6	Elephant	3	4
7	Icky Thump	3	4
8	Broken boy soldiers	3	4

Artist

Artist_ID	Name	DoB	Town	Nationality
1	Dido	25-12-71	London	English
2	Adele	5-5-1988	London	English
3	White Stripes	1997	Detroit	American

Label

Label_ID	Name
1	RCA
2	Sony Music
3	Aristo
4	XL

5.4 PRIMARY, SECONDARY AND FOREIGN KEYS

Notice how the CD table has a unique value for each CD. This unique field
which I've called **CD_ID** is the **primary key**. The two other tables holding
data on artists and labels also have their own unique primary key which I've
called **Artist_ID** and **Label_ID** respectively.

The tables are linked via their primary keys. Look at the first entry in the
CD table. The first CD_ID, i.e. number 1 has title 'Safe trip home' and
is by the artist with Artist_ID 1. We can see who this is by looking in the
artist table to find that artist number 1 is Dido. Similarly, by looking at the
label table we can see that this CD is on the label with Label_ID 1, i.e. RCA.

The second entry has the title 'Girl who got away' and is also by the same artist, i.e. Dido but is on label with ID 2 which from the third table we can see is Sony Music.

When a primary key in one table is placed in a second table to link the tables together it is called a **foreign key** in the second table. In our example, the two IDs, Artist_ID and Label_ID which are primary keys in their own tables are foreign keys in the CD table.

Occasionally we may want to have a second primary key in a table. This usually happens when we want to sort the table in some other order than by primary key. A second key used in this way is called a **secondary key**.

A teacher uses a database to store the marks of pupils from all year 9 classes. PUPIL and CLASS are two entities used in this database. Explain the term entity. [A451 Jan 2011 Q7 (2)]

- A real world object
- . . . about which data is stored in a database
- Entities correspond to tables in the database

Mrs Smith runs a dog sitting service that looks after dogs whose owners are going away on holiday. Mrs Smith uses a database with two tables.

- **The table DOG stores the following data about each dog: DogID, name, sex, weight, date of arrival, date of departure.**
- **The table JOB stores the daily jobs that she needs to do with each dog.**

An extract of the JOB table is shown below.

JobNumber	DogID	JobType	Time	Details
35	SM13	Feed	Morning	250g of Hundex
36	BA12	Walk	Afternoon	At least 30 minutes
37	SM13	Walk	Afternoon	Keep on leash
38	GH14	Other	Morning	Medicine: 1 tablet of Depuchine
39	HT19	Other	Evening	Brush fur

Explain why DogID has been included in this table. [A451 Jan 2012 Q6 (3)]

- It is used as a foreign key in this table
- . . . and is the primary key of the DOG table
- It is used to link the two tables

- ... and allows us to find the details of the dog to which each job relates and it means that we do not need to re-enter dog details for each job

A teacher uses a database to store the marks of pupils from all year 9 classes. PUPIL and CLASS are two entities used in this database. The data for the first four pupils in the PUPIL table is shown below.

PupilNumber	Surname	FirstName	ClassCode
A01	Adams	Michelle	9DK
A02	Ali	Mohammed	9BH
A03	Ali	Shirelle	9DK
A04	Azor	Michelle	9FT

State the primary key for the PUPIL table and explain your answer. [A451 Jan 2011 Q7 (3)]

- Primary Key: PupilNumber
- Because it is a unique identifier
- Two pupils cannot have the same PupilNumber
- ... but they can have the same Surname, FirstName or ClassCode

The database also contains a CLASS table. The primary key for the CLASS table is ClassCode. Explain why ClassCode has also been included in the PUPIL table. (3)

- ClassCode is used here as a foreign key
- ... to link CLASS and PUPIL
- Using ClassCode, all the class details can be retrieved from the Class table
- ... otherwise the class details will have to be rewritten every time to avoid data redundancy

A television set top box contains a database of television channels and programmes. Data about television channels are stored in the CHANNEL table. Part of this table is shown below.

ChannelID	ChannelName	ChannelType	Broadcaster	HD
346	ETV News	News	ETV	False
347	Screen One	Movies	ETV	True
349	BLING one	General	Bling	True
350	Vivo	Documentary	ETV	False
351	Nature	Documentary	Bling	False
355	Screen One	Movies	Bling	True

State the primary key for the CHANNEL table and give a reason for your choice (1,1)

- Primary key: ChannelID

- It is a unique identifier, two channels can have the same ChannelName but they cannot have the same ChannelID

Data about programmes that will be broadcast are stored in the PROGRAMME table. The data about each programme includes the channel on which it would be broadcast. Explain how a foreign key can be used to connect the PROGRAMME table to the CHANNEL table. (2)

- ChannelID is the primary key of the CHANNEL table
- ...and can be stored in the PROGRAMME table
- ...where it is a foreign key

Explain why the programme data is stored in a separate table from the channel data. (3)

- Less data entry is required
- ...because programme and channel details are only stored once
- It avoids redundancy because we don't have to repeat channel details for every programme on that channel
- It avoids inconsistency (for example, when channel data changes)

Once we have constructed our database which may consist of a number of separate tables linked by keys, we will usually want to put information into the database. We usually use **forms** to do this. When properly designed, forms are a simple, intuitive way of entering data into a database. They usually consist of an input screen which allows data items to be entered, displayed and edited before submission. They often make use of features such as drop down lists, checkboxes and radio buttons to make it easier for the user to enter data and to ensure that no information is missed. They can also be designed to 'validate' the information to ensure that data is in the correct form before it is submitted to the database. When all of the data has been entered satisfactorily, the user will usually press a 'submit' button to update the database with the new information.

Once we have a populated database, full of useful information the next step is usually to pull information out of it. To do so, we submit **queries** to the database. Queries are simply questions written in a particular format that we want the database to answer. After submitting our query to the database we typically want the information that we have extracted from the database to be presented to us in a neat, orderly fashion in the form of a **report**.

Let's return to our three tables which make up our relational database of our (very) small CD collection (shown again below).

CD

CD_ID	Title	Artist_ID	Label_ID
1	Safe trip home	1	1
2	Girl who got away	1	2
3	White flag	1	3
4	Cold shoulder	2	4
5	Home town glory	2	4
6	Elephant	3	4
7	Icky Thump	3	4
8	Broken boy soldiers	3	4

Artist

Artist_ID	Name	DoB	Town	Nationality
1	Dido	25-12-71	London	English
2	Adele	5-5-1988	London	English
3	White Stripes	1997	Detroit	American

Label

Label_ID	Name
1	RCA
2	Sony Music
3	Aristo
4	XL

A typical query might ask for all the artists that are English. We might want a **report** printed which showed these artists together with some relevant information including a list of CD titles in alphabetical order. Having queried our database we would expect to see a simple report something along the lines shown below.

```
                    CD COLLECTION

                    25 Mar 2013

        Dido        Girl who got away        Sony Music
                    Safe trip home           RCA
                    White flag               Aristo


        Born :      London 25 Dec 1971


        Adele       Cold shoulder            XL
                    Home from glory          XL


        Born :      London 5 May 1988
```

Note that we have a title on our report together with the date that the report was printed. Each English artist (in our case there are only two) is listed in turn together with the titles and labels of their CDs in ascending alphabetical order. As an extra touch, the report also adds where and when the artist was born.

Mrs Smith runs a dog sitting service that looks after dogs whose owners are going away on holiday. Mrs Smith uses a database with two tables.

- **The table DOG stores the following data about each dog: DogID, name, sex, weight, date of arrival, date of departure.**
- **The table JOB stores the daily jobs that she needs to do with each dog.**

An extract of the JOB table is shown below.

JobNumber	DogID	JobType	Time	Details
35	SM13	Feed	Morning	250g of Hundex
36	BA12	Walk	Afternoon	At least 30 minutes
37	SM13	Walk	Afternoon	Keep on leash
38	GH14	Other	Morning	Medicine: 1 tablet of Depuchine
39	HT19	Other	Evening	Brush fur

Mrs Smith wants to use database management software to create a report of all the jobs that she needs to perform on any given day, using data from the DOG and JOB tables. In the space below, design a layout for the report. [A451 Jan 2012 Q6 (6)]

The examiners needed you to include the following details on your drawing.

- There is a title
- There is a date
- Jobs are grouped/sorted appropriately (e.g. by dog, time or job type)
- Each job includes the Dog Name
- Each job includes the Dog ID
- Each Job includes the Job type
- Each job includes details

The following report was the sort of thing that they had in mind.

JOBS

Monday   21 May 2012

Morning

| Bob | SM13 | Feed | 250g of Hundex |
| Cyfaill | GH14 | Other | Medicine: 1 tablet of Depuchine |

Afternoon

| Bob | SM13 | Walk | Keep on leash |
| Cymro | BA12 | Walk | At least 30 minutes |

Evening

| Honey | HT19 | Other | Brush fur |

A grocery shop uses a database with a DBMS to keep records of its stock. The database uses forms and reports. Describe each of these and give one example of how it would be used in the shop's database. [A451 Jun 2011 Q2 (3,3)]

- Form
  - An input screen
  - ...allowing the chosen data items to be displayed and edited
  - Forms use text boxes, drop down lists, checkboxes etc.
  - When edited, the changes are updated in the database
  - Any suitable example from the shop e.g. a form to enter new products

- Report
  - An output of the data in a database
  - A snapshot of the data at a given time, when printed
  - ...of specified fields, laid out in a specified format
  - Aggregates may be calculated and displayed
  - Any suitable example from the shop e.g. report of weekly sales

Earlier we said that we could generate reports from databases by framing a question in the right format and then querying the database. The 'right format' for many databases is to frame our queries according to the rules of the **Structured Query Language** or SQL. This language is used by Microsoft Access behind the scenes when you set up and delete tables, add and delete fields and so on. It also runs when you set up your queries and it is perfectly possible to use SQL directly.

The examiners do not need you to be familiar with SQL but they do want you to understand how the use of logical operators such as AND, OR and NOT can be used when framing database queries. The type of questions that they ask are intended to check that you understand how to use logical operators and what results are expected when a given question is asked.

For example, if we return to Mrs Smith's dog sitting service question.

Mrs Smith runs a dog sitting service that looks after dogs whose owners are going away on holiday. Mrs Smith uses a database with two tables.

- **The table DOG stores the following data about each dog: DogID, name, sex, weight, date of arrival, date of departure.**
- **The table JOB stores the daily jobs that she needs to do with each dog.**

An extract of the JOB table is shown below.

JobNumber	DogID	JobType	Time	Details
35	SM13	Feed	Morning	250g of Hundex
36	BA12	Walk	Afternoon	At least 30 minutes
37	SM13	Walk	Afternoon	Keep on leash
38	GH14	Other	Morning	Medicine: 1 tablet of Depuchine
39	HT19	Other	Evening	Brush fur

Mrs Smith uses a query to select jobs using the following criteria

(Time = Afternoon) OR (Time = Evening)

List the JobNumbers of the jobs that will be selected from the extract shown. [A451 Jan 2012 Q6 (1)]

- 36, 37, 39 because clearly these three jobs need to be done in either the afternoon OR the evening

A grocery shop uses a database with a DBMS to keep records of its stock. Here is some data from the supermarket's database.

ID	Description	Supplier	Amount left	Reorder level	Discontinued	Price
0001	6 eggs	Hill Farm	50	20	FALSE	£0.98
0002	2 litres of milk	Hill Farm	17	20	TRUE	£1.20
0003	1kg apples	Killey's	42	50	FALSE	£0.79
0004	250g butter	Hill Farm	12	25	FALSE	£0.49
0005	500g Moku Flakes	Moku Foods	0	10	TRUE	£0.99
0006	6 salad tomatoes	Killey's	30	30	FALSE	£0.89
0007	580g can baked beans	Moku Foods	27	30	FALSE	£0.42
0008	Family tomato ketchup	Moku Foods	41	20	FALSE	£1.45

The shop runs queries using logical operators to select data for different purposes. State the ProductID of the products in the above sample which fit the following criteria. (a) Supplier = Killey's, (b) Price > £1.00 OR Supplier = Hill Farm [A451 Jun 2011 Q2 (1,3)]

Supplier = Killey's

- Answer: 0003, 0006 (1 mark is awarded if both answers are present and there are no others)

Price > £1.00 OR Supplier = Hill Farm

- Answer: 0001, 0002, 0004, 0008
- ...1 mark awarded if 0001, 0002, 0004 are all in answer
- ...1 mark if 0002 and 0008 are in answer
- ...1 mark if 0002 is not repeated and there are extra answers

Write the criteria which can be used to select all products which are not discontinued and where the QuantityLeft is lower than the ReorderLevel. (3)

- Discontinued = False
- AND
- Quantity Left < Reorder Level

Validation

When entering data into a database it is a very good precaution to try to ensure that the data being entered is sensible. For example if you are asked to enter the age of a student, a value of 819 would clearly be nonsense given that the oldest person recorded in recent times has not lived longer than 130. Similarly, if a user is entering his name and we find that his name runs to over 100 characters, it's unlikely that he's entering his real name. Checking for sensible input is called **validating** the input. Validating doesn't guarantee that the data being entered is true, but it does check that it is reasonable and complete. There are a variety of standard validation checks that can be carried out and they include the following.

Presence check: – is the data present, i.e. has the field been filled?

Length check: – is the data of a reasonable length? For example, is a username between 5 and 15 characters long?

Format check: – is the data of the correct format? For example, a date might need to be in the form dd/mm/yyyy

Range check: – is data in the correct range? For example, a pensioner is someone over the age of 65 and (presumably) younger than say 130.

Existence check: – does the data that has been entered match a previously recorded value. For example, does entering flight code AZ854 match a flight that actually exists.

OK - back to Mrs Smith's dog sitting service again for one last time.

Mrs Smith runs a dog sitting service that looks after dogs whose owners are going away on holiday. Mrs Smith uses a database with two tables.

- **The table DOG stores the following data about each dog: DogID, name, sex, weight, date of arrival, date of departure.**
- **The table JOB stores the daily jobs that she needs to do with each dog.**

The DOG table contains fields for the sex and weight of the dog. Describe a validation check that can be done on the sex field. [A451 Jan 2012 Q6 (2)]

- Existence check
- Male or Female is allowed
- ... and no other entry in this field is possible

Describe a different validation check that can be done on the weight field. (2)

- Range check

- The weight must be a (real) number
- ...and must be positive

A dentist uses a database to store the details of patients and their appointments. A database management system (DBMS) is used which includes forms, queries and reports. Tick one box in each row to show whether each of the following statements best describes a form, a query or a report. [A451 Specimen Paper 2010 Q11 (3)]

	Form	Query	Report
This can be used to print out all the appointments that the dentist has booked			
This can be used to enter a patient's details when the patient registers with the dentist			
This can be used to find out all the appointments that a certain patient has made			

Answer:

	Form	Query	Report
This can be used to print out all the appointments that the dentist has booked			✓
This can be used to enter a patient's details when the patient registers with the dentist	✓		
This can be used to find out all the appointments that a certain patient has made		✓	

Justify the use of separate entities to store the patient and appointment data. (3)

- The patients data does not have to be repeated for each appointment
- ...as the patient ID can be stored with the appointment to link the two entities
- Allows the patient (and appointment data) to be manipulated independently e.g. if the name of the patient changes
- Avoids the possibility of the patient data becoming inconsistent due to being stored multiple times

When a patient makes an appointment, the start time of the appointment needs to be validated. State two validation checks which can be carried out on the start time of the appointment. (2)

- The time is in the correct format / hh:mm
- The time is within the dentists working day
- The hours are in the range 1 – 12 or 0 – 24
- The minutes are in the range 0 – 59

Computer networks and communications

6.1 NETWORKS

A network *"is a linked set of computer systems, which may be capable of sharing computer power and resources such as printers, CD-ROM and DVD drives and databases"*[1]. The computer systems may connected by wire, wirelessly, via microwave links, via the Public Switch Telephone Network (PSTN), by satellite links or by a combination of all of the above.

Networking Advantages and Disadvantages

There are significant advantages to be gained by connecting computer systems together. At the most basic level, it is possible to share expensive resources such as printers, plotters, scanners or very large hard disks. Once computers are connected it is then possible using suitable software for users to communicate with one another, sharing files, exchanging gossip and so on.

One clear disadvantage is that once users are able to communicate with each other and share files and data, it is much more difficult to keep information secure. Additionally, it's very easy to pick up computer viruses all of which can compromise security and potentially damage computer systems.

A small business has three stand-alone computers, a printer and an internet connection in an office.

State two advantages of connecting the computers to create a local area network. [A451 Jan 2011 Q2 (2)]

- To share the printer
- To share the internet connection

---

[1]British Computer Society Glossary of Computing and ICT

- To share files
- To communicate with each other e.g. by email

A classroom in a primary school has 6 stand alone computers. The school decides to connect them to form a LAN. What is a LAN?
[A451 Specimen Paper 2010 Q6 (1)]

- Local Area Network
- A network which covers a small area like a building

State two advantages of connecting the computers into a LAN. (2)

- Can share files
- Can share resources (e.g. printer)
- Computers can be managed/controlled centrally
- Users/computers can communicate with each other

Network Hardware

To connect computers together requires a variety of different hardware depending on how close the computers are to one another. If the computers are all in a large room, it's very easy to wire them together. Modern wiring lets data move at up to 1 Gbit per second. Alternatively, if the network needs to connect computers in a number of rooms, wireless connections may be possible. These run quite a bit slower than wired with 108 MBits per second being fairly common. For greater distances it is possible to use the telephone network and for greater distances again, it is possible, though very expensive to use satellites. It is a little known fact that the countries of the world are connected via wire cables running across both them and any oceans that lie in between. For instance there are many cables running across both the Atlantic and Pacific oceans carrying data between Europe and the USA and the USA and the Far East respectively. The following map[2] shows where the major submarine cables are currently laid.

---

[2]http://gatech.wikidot.com/non-network-attacks-against-infrastructure

The internet's undersea world

Wired connections need wires, network cards and switches or hubs. The **wires** are typically Cat-5, i.e. four twisted pairs of cables inside a shielded metal sheath inside a plastic outer cable. These connect to computer systems via RJ-45 plug connectors. The network cards are usually incorporated onto the motherboards of modern computers and are visible only via the RJ-45 connector on the outside of the casing. A **hub** allows two or more computers to pass data to each other. The hub can only deal with one connection at a time and it slows down considerably if it is connected to many computers, each of which is trying to talk to others. A **switch** is an intelligent hub and is capable of handing many connections simultaneously. Switches are much more appropriate in offices and schools where many computers are connected and are sending data simultaneously.

Wireless connections need appropriate hardware to broadcast and receive wireless data. The hardware is normally found on the motherboard in modern laptops and computer systems, sending and receiving data is usually simply a matter of switching it on and connecting to the nearest **Wireless Access Point (WAP)**. A WAP is essentially a hub that allows wireless connections.

If you're connecting to the Internet via the telephone network you'll need some form of . Routers are "sophisticated switched hubs. They hold information about the addresses of computers attached to the network and can forward data efficiently to the correct location via an appropriate route"[3]. You'll also need a **modem** which converts the incoming digital information from the computer to analog signals that are then sent down the telephone cable. The word modem is short for modulator-demodulator since it can

---

[3]British Computer Society Glossary of Computing and ICT

modulate (encode digital information in the voice frequency range of an analogue telephone signal) and demodulate, i.e. recover the digital information
from an analog signal. Clearly in any data exchange across the telephone
network a modem is required at both ends.

Peer-to-Peer and Client-Server networks

We will look at physical connections in the next section, but computer connections also need to be thought of in a more conceptual way, in how the
computers are organised.

Networks in which each computer is as important as any other are called
peer-to-peer networks. In such networks, each computer, although connected to others on the network conceptually stands alone. One computer
may have a printer connected to it and may share that printer with others
on the network. Another may be connected to the Internet and will share
the connection with all others on the network, but no computer is 'in charge'
of the network. Users log in to their own computers, they save their files on
their computer, have their own unique desktop and so on. The BCS Glossary
describes a peer-to-peer network as *"a simple network that provides shared
resources, such as printers and storage, but may offer little else in the way
of additional facilities such as file security"*. Home networks are typical examples of peer-to-peer networks.

An alternative form of organisation is that of a **client-server** network. In
this configuration, the network is organised around one or more servers. Each
server has a particular role to play. One server will maintain a database of
users, passwords, usernames and access rights. Users of client computers,
(computers that are not servers) are required to log in to the server and
authenticate themselves using their username and password before they are
allowed to use the computer. There may be additional servers on the network to handle printing and file serving, though these tasks are commonly
undertaken by a single server. In order to provide these services, servers run
special versions of a given operating system. These versions are usually quite
expensive which is why they are almost never used in home networks.

In addition to proving authentication, print and file services, servers usually
provide centralised back up services, centralised control of security and anti-
virus facilities and a host of other other services transparent to the client
machine users. In the case of schools, servers often operate a filtering system
whereby access to Internet sites deemed unsuitable for viewing in school is

controlled.

Network topologies

Computer networks can be physically connected in a variety of ways, the technical description for which is **network topology**. (Topology is the mathematical study of space, and in particular of how space is connected). There are three common topologies used to describe computer networks. The three diagrams below show each of these.

In the first, a **bus** network, the computers are connected by T-pieces (see diagram) or short pieces of cable called **spurs** to a much longer cable. The main cable, the bus has **terminators** at both ends. Terminators ensure that the signals are absorbed and do not reflect back down the cable. The bus is usually a **coaxial** cable. A coaxial cable consists of a centre wire surrounded by insulation and then by a grounded shield of braided wire. The shield minimises electrical and radio frequency interference.

Describe, using a diagram, how the computers can be connected to each other using a bus topology, stating what hardware will be needed. (6)

The examiners were looking for a diagram such as the one shown that showed most and ideally all of the following components.

- Terminators are shown at each end of bus
- Bus line is shown
- 3 computers are shown attached to a bus
- A printer is attached to the bus or to a computer
- The Internet connection is connected to a router or to a computer
- Network adapters are needed on each computer
- A router is needed to share the Internet connection
- Cables are needed to connect the different devices
- Note : Hub or switch is acceptable only if it is clear that there is a logical bus IN the hub or switch

Bus Network

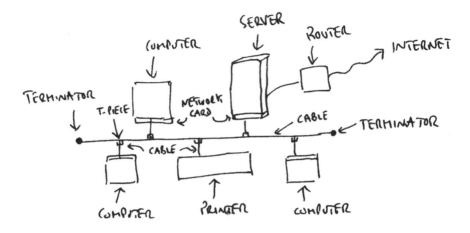

The second diagram shows a **ring** network. This is essentially a bus network with no terminators. Instead the two end points of the cable are joined. Computers attach to the bus either via T-pieces or spurs. Coaxial cable is usually the preferred choice for this type of network.

Ring Network

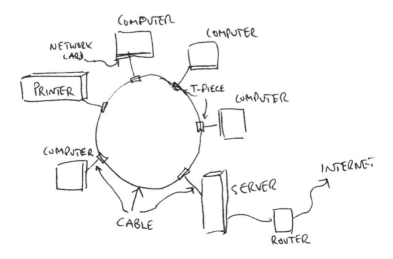

The third diagram shows a wired **star** network. In this topology, all of the network devices are connected to a central hub or switch by cables, usually Cat-5. In a wireless setup the switch or hub would be replaced by a **Wireless Access Point (WAP)**, the network cards replaced by Wi-fi adaptors and the cables removed.

Star Network

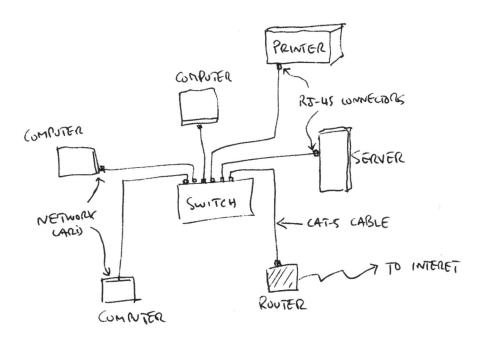

A school wishes to use a star topology for its LAN. Explain, with reasons, what additional hardware will be required to connect the computers into a LAN. [A451 Specimen Paper 2010 Q6 (4)]

- The star topology requires all workstations to be connected to a central point
- ...so a hub/switch is needed
- The computers need to be physically or wirelessly connected to the hub
- ...so cables and network interface cards
- ...or a wireless access point and WiFi adapters will be needed

There are various advantages and disadvantages of each of these topologies. If a break occurs in the cable in the case of bus and ring networks, since signals cannot pass through a break in the physical cable, all computers on the network will be affected. In the case of a star network, if one of the cables is broken, only the computer that is attached to the hub or switch via that cable will be affected. Coaxial cable is also expensive. Star networks require more cabling since each computer has its own cable back to the hub or switch, but these cables are usually relatively inexpensive.

A school decides to use a star topology to create a LAN. Describe what is meant by a star topology. You may use a diagram. [A451 Specimen Paper 2010 Q6 (2)]

- A hub / server at the centre of the network
- All computers attached to the hub/server
- Resources (e.g. printer) can also be attached to hub/server
- An appropriate diagram to represent this information is also acceptable

LAN or WAN?

A **Local Area Network** (LAN) is a network in which the computers are situated close to one another. A typical example would be a school, business or university complex. Computers are connected via coaxial and Cat-5 cables and/or wirelessly. Data transfer around the network is usually fast at up to 1 GBit per second.

A **Wide Area Network** (WAN) is a network in which the computer systems are distributed over a wide area. They are connected via the telephone lines, via microwave links, submarine cables or satellite. Data transfer via these links can be fast in the case of cables and microwave links, but considerably slower when travelling through the telephone lines or via satellite. International companies with offices in various countries whose computers are all connected are examples of the use of Wide Area Networks. The Internet which is the network of networks is the ultimate example of a WAN.

A city has many libraries. Each library has several computers. All the computers in a library are connected to each other through a local area network (LAN) and the libraries are connected through a wide area network (WAN). In the table below, tick one box in each row to show whether the statements are true for the LAN only or for both LAN and WAN. [A451 Specimen Paper 2012 Q1 (4)]

	LAN only	Both LAN and WAN
This can be used to check the books in another library		
This can be used to send messages between the libraries		
This will include a printer where users can print results of a search		
Protocols are needed to allow the computers to communicate		

Answer:

	LAN only	Both LAN and WAN
This can be used to check the books in another library		✓
This can be used to send messages between the libraries		✓
This will include a printer where users can print results of a search	✓	
Protocols are needed to allow the computers to communicate		✓

IP, MAC, packets and protocols

In order for any computer to communicate with any other computer there needs to be an agreed set of rules to enable the communication to take place. To explain what this means, imagine that two people are having a conversation. One will speak whilst the other listens. At some point the first speaker may pause and the second speaker will seize his opportunity and will say something. The first speaker will listen. At some point whilst the second speaker is speaking, the first speaker may shrug, make some gesture with his hand or otherwise indicate that she'd like to say something. The second speaker stops and the first speaker takes over the conversation. This is a ordinary conversation, but without realising it, both speakers are following an agreed set of protocols. Unless agitated, both speakers wait their turn, indicating the need to speak by making or saying some gesture which informs the other speaker that they wish to say something. Young children have little understanding initially of how conversations are conducted and are forever being told to 'wait their turn', not to be 'rude' and so on. Children gradually and without being aware of the learning process eventually learn the rules of polite conversation.

Computer systems don't learn in the way we do. Instead they are programmed how to communicate. They are given a set of rules. These rules are called **protocols**. A simple example might be the following.

Computer A wishes to send data to computer B. Computer A first sends a packet of information which computer B correctly interprets as a request to communicate. Computer B sends back a packet saying that's it ready to listen. Computer A responds with a stream of information. Computer B is being overwhelmed and sends a packet which asks computer A to stop momentarily. Computer A does so and resumes when computer B sends another packet asking computer A to restart. And so the dialogue continues.

This is all very well, but how do computers A and B identify each other? If there are many computers on the network how does computer A know which computer is computer B? The answer lies in addresses. Each computer on the network must have a unique address within the network. Each address is made up of 32 bits. 32 bits is 4 bytes and as you know, each byte can hold a number from 0 – 255. Rather then remembering a 32 bit computer address in binary format, it's much easier to divide it up into four bytes each of which is separated by a dot and written in denary rather than binary.

For example, consider the 32 bit address 11000000101010000000000100001110.

If you look very carefully, this is made up of four bytes of 11000000, 10101000, 00000001 and 00001110. These bytes represent the denary numbers 192, 168, 1 and 14, so the usual way of writing the address of this computer is 192.168.1.14. This address is called the IP address. IP is short for **Internet Protocol** and refers to the fact that addresses of this type are part of the Internet Protocol, i.e. the set of rules for how computers are addressed on the Internet. In addition to its IP address, each networkable device has a **Media Access Control or MAC** address. Whereas IP addresses are 32 bits long, MAC addresses are 48 bits, meaning that there are 2^{48} or $281,474,976,710,656$ possible MAC addresses. This very large number uniquely identifies every device anywhere in the world. You might ask, so, why have two unique addresses? If the IP address is unique, why have MAC addresses as well?

There are good reasons which hark back to when the various protocols were being created. These reasons are not important but MAC addresses are hard coded into the device itself and never change. An IP address on the other hand is not built into the device and is normally acquired, usually by asking a **Dynamic Host Control Protocol or DHCP** computer for an IP address. The school router which allows connections within a school to the internet acquires its unique IP address from its Internet Service Provider (ISP). It in turn allocates unique (within the school network) addresses to each of the computers on the network each time they are switched on.

A similar situation exists for smartphones. Each smartphone is given a unique IP address from the DHCP server at the carrier, i.e. O2, 3, Vodaphone etc. The IP address may change during the course of the day but this is transparent to the user.

So, all computers can be uniquely identified by the IP addresses. When they talk to each other what do they send? They send **packets**. Packets are collections of bytes, typically around 1,500 bytes long. The format of a packet is precisely defined and in particular, each packet has the address of the sending computer and the address of where the packet is going written on it. 'Inside' the packet is the data together with a **checksum**. A checksum is a simple error detection scheme where a calculation is made on the data and the result sent along with the packet. The receiving computer performs the same calculation on the data and if the result is the same as the checksum sent with the data, the data can be assumed to have been received correctly.

Whenever a computer wishes to send data to another on the network, or indeed to any other computer in the world, it chops up its data into packet-sized chunks, puts the first chunk of data into a packet, calculates the checksum, puts the address of where each packet is going to, puts its own address on the packet, writes the packet number (for example, packet 17 out of 250) and sends it off. The receiving computer gets each packet, opens it to get at the data and recalculates the checksum. If it gets the same answer as the checksum in the packet, it knows that the packet has been received correctly.

Since it is likely that the the packet arriving at a computer is in fact one of possibly many hundreds of packets making up the data that has been sent, the receiving computer also has to recombine data from each of the many packets. If any packet has been corrupted en route, a packet is sent back to the original computer asking for the data to be resent.

This is called **packet switching**. Although it is not the only way of sending data from computer to computer, with the advent of the Internet, it is by far the most common.

Network Security

Standalone computers, unconnected to anything else can be placed in stain-
less steel rooms inside concrete bunkers underneath 100 metres of rock. Such
computers are fairly secure. The moment you connect computers to other
computes, security becomes a major issue. Aside from the risk from viruses
and hackers as explained on pages 47 - 48, there are the more mundane issues
where users may want to keep their personal files private, system administrators may want to control access to important system files and students
do not want their homework visible to other students. These issues can be
controlled by the sensible use of **user access levels**, **passwords** and **encryption** techniques.

Some users are clearly more important in a network sense than others. System administrators need to able to do anything on a network. They may
need to install software, modify important system files, set up users and perform a whole host of often complicated network related tasks. Consequently,
system administrators need to have system wide access. An ordinary user
meanwhile has the right to have their data kept private from other ordinary
users, though clearly not from the system administrator. Users may belong
to groups, for example in a school setting there are students and there are
staff. A maths teacher would belong to the group STAFF, a student in year
11 would naturally belong to the group STUDENTS. Members of STAFF
might have access to important information on student family information
and exam results, members of STUDENT might have access to a shared area
for storing files, club activities and so on. User access levels can be assigned
on a user level and on group levels. John Smith, a physics teacher would have
his own private area for documents relevant to his department and as a member of STAFF he would also have access to STAFF areas. Emily Thompson,
a student in year 9 would have a private area for her homework and access
to any STUDENT areas. Bob Ainsworth the systems administrator would
have access to everything.

The system administrator is responsible for implementing appropriate user
access levels on instruction from whomever ultimately controls or owns the
network, the headmistress or headmaster in the case of a school, the managing director in the case of a company. Each user is usually given a unique
username and password combination which is used to authenticate them on
the network. When a given user logs in using their username and password,
user access levels appropriate to them are set and they are then free to roam
the network at their particular level.

To prevent unauthorised access from outside of a network the router often runs a **firewall**. This is a program which monitors all traffic into and out of the router. Since all packets between the network and the outside world must first travel through the router this means that nothing can pass between the network and the outside world without being scrutinised. For further information on firewalls refer to page 48.

As a further aid to network security, important files may be **encrypted**. Encryption is the conversion of a file into a secret set of codes according to some (usually very complex) mathematical computer algorithm. Encrypting data is probably the most effective means of providing data security but only if the encryption algorithms are sufficiently secure. To decrypt a file, one must have the secret code or password. Without it, some encryption algorithms simply cannot be broken.

Finally, most companies require their employees to sign a binding legal document assuring the company that the employee will take all reasonable precautions in their use of data on the network. Such agreements will include clauses where the employee agree that they will abide by company policy regarding the downloading of material from the Internet and that they will abide by the provisions of the data protection act.

A large company with 200 employees uses a local area network (LAN) which includes all the computers in its head office. Describe the security measures and network policies which can be used to safeguard the security and privacy of the company's data on the network. The quality of written communication will be assessed in your answer to this question. [A451 Jun 2011 Q8 (6)]

The examiners were expecting you to make the following points.

- Physical security measures – computers and servers should be placed in locked rooms and there should be lock down cables for laptops
- Firewalls should allow only authorised access to the network and only authorised users and/or programs should be allowed to share data out of the network
- User groups & access levels – different users should be given rights to different data according their responsibility and the need to protect privacy
- Passwords should be enforced – they should be strong and changed regularly to ensure privacy and protect files from being accessed by malicious hackers

- Data on the network should be encrypted
- There should be strong encrypted WiFi security if WiFi is used
- Employees should be required to sign an acceptable use policy as part of their contract to ensure they do not put the data at risk of corruption/abide by data protection legislation/do not give the data to third parties etc.

A city has many libraries. Each library has several computers. All the computers in a library are connected to each other through a local area network (LAN) and the libraries are connected through a wide area network (WAN). Some computers are available for public use. Explain why the libraries need the following security measures.

User access levels [A451 Specimen Paper 2012 Q1 (2)]

- Different users should only have permissions to files/areas/services of the network
- ... which they actually need
- E.g. the public should only be able to search
- E.g. only employees should issue books
- E.g. only managers can look at pay records
- To prevent malicious or accidental corruption of parts of the network

Firewalls (2)

- Stops all access to/from the WAN
- ... unless it has been authorised
- E.g. requests from other libraries
- Prevents hackers
- ... from compromising the system

Network Policies

Network policies is a blanket term used by examiners to cover policies on acceptable use, disaster recovery, failover, backup and archiving.

An **acceptable use** policy refers to a set of rules that the manager or owner of a network of computer systems uses to restrict the ways in which the network may be used. Many schools and institutions have such policies in place so that students and employees for example are perhaps not allowed to use the network for personal use, or perhaps accessing and downloading illegal material from the Internet. Many, perhaps most students regard it as perfectly acceptable to download software, music and video from the Internet for their own personal use. Unless otherwise indicated, such downloads are invariably illegal and a school which allowed such downloading would soon find itself in great difficulty explaining to the relevant authorities why it allowed such illegal activities. It is no defence to say that it didn't know. Each school and institution has a legal obligation to ensure that its students or employees do not make use of its network facilities for illegal ends.

It is common for schools and companies to insist that their students and employees sign an acceptable use policy document before joining the school or company.

All schools and companies will need to put in place some form of **disaster recovery** policy so that if or when disaster strikes, perhaps in the form of a fire or flood, or simply catastrophic computer failure, important files and data are kept safe. Today this usually means some form of off site storage of important files and data. Data is copied daily to an off site location either directly, often over the Internet, or indirectly via a hard disk or DVD so that if disaster strikes, the data can be restored relatively quickly.

Effective disaster recovery starts with prevention so far as that can be achieved. Measures to prevent disaster might include

- mirroring data on the servers so that in case of hard disk failure a second disk will also have a copy of the data

- surge protection so that in the case of sudden high voltage spikes in supply sensitive equipment is protected

- fire extinguishers and alarms

- uninterruptible power supplies attached to the most important systems so that in case of power loss, power can be maintained for an hour or two while efforts are made to restore power

- firewalls and anti-virus software to prevent data damage through hacking or virus attack

- **failover** in which a second redundant or standby computer system takes over (usually) automatically if the first system fails. An institution that takes disaster prevention measures seriously might have copies of each of its important servers running in parallel with the originals. The original and the copy are connected and all activity is duplicated on both the original and the copy. In situations where the original server fails, the copy simply takes over. An analogy in the human world might be that of pilot and co-pilot on a commercial aircraft. If the pilot is suddenly incapacitated, the co-pilot simply takes over.

All computer systems should be **backed up** on a regular basis, once a day is perfectly common. On a well administered system an initial copy of all data is made and on subsequent occasions any **changes** to the data, not normally the data itself, is copied to the backup device. Whilst the initial backup will normally be very slow owing to the very large amount of data to be copied, subsequent backups will be very much quicker. If data is lost, the backups can be used to restore the original data. Backups are normally taken off-site in case of fire and if it is absolutely essential that data is not lost, multiple backups can be made and stored in various locations.

On a regular, but not frequent basis, perhaps every six months, perhaps every year in the case of many schools, data is **archived**. Archiving is the copying of data that is no longer required on a day to day basis, but which for various reasons, often legal, must be kept safe. Copying such data to suitable DVDs, hard disks, or to some other company's data storage facilities means that the data can then be removed from the original system, thus freeing up system resources.

6.2 THE INTERNET

The Internet is everywhere. The dream of total connectivity is close - everyone, anywhere is now potentially capable of communicating with anyone, everywhere. This section looks at what the Internet is, what it is made up of, some of the important technologies that make it work and a little about where it might be headed.

A Network of Networks

The clearest description of the Internet is that it is the network of networks. The world is full of local and wide area networks. There are networks at home, in schools, in colleges and universities, in businesses and in government. The Internet is the network that connects all of those networks, plus millions of other computer systems dedicated to handling emails, web pages, file transfers, blogs, images, video and sound. The world wide web is a subset of the Internet. A computer system is part of the world wide web if it **serves** web pages, i.e. makes web pages available to the user. The Internet is much more than simply web pages.

The table below contains some statements about the internet. Tick one box in each row to show whether each statement is true or false.
[A451 Jan 2012 Q4 (3)]

	TRUE	FALSE
The internet is the same as the World Wide Web		
The internet is a Local Area Network		
The internet is a network between many networks		

Answer

	TRUE	FALSE
The internet is the same as the World Wide Web		✓
The internet is a Local Area Network		✓
The internet is a network between many networks	✓	

Internet Hardware

For the Internet to work, it needs many millions of routers. Routers can be small dedicated boxes or normal computer systems running appropriate software. Their job is to take the packet that started life at your computer, take a look at where it is trying to get to, and then make a decision as to which router would be the most likely to take your packet closer to its final destination. Routes are often highly congested and each router will take congestion into account before sending the packet off. Each router between you and your ultimate destination makes such a decision until eventually, usually in a matter of milliseconds, after passing through many tens or possibly hundreds of routers, your message gets to its destination.

Note that if you're sending a large email message or downloading a video file or song, the data is too large to fit into a single packet which is normally only around 1,500 bytes long. Consequently, the video file is split into as many packets as are necessary. Each packet is sent onto the Internet and **finds its own way** to the destination via the routers. For example if you were downloading a video from a server in California in the USA, some packets might get back to you via Tokyo, Beijing, Bombay, Tehran, Jerusalem, Rome, Paris and London, while others might go via Chicago, Dublin and Cardiff.

In addition to the millions of routers, the Internet also needs untold miles of cabling, ranging across continents and under the seas, backed up by wireless facilities via microwave links and satellite. At home, you'll need a modem and a router to access your Internet Service Provider or ISP. They'll need the same at their end.

DNS Servers

Another integral part of the web is the **Domain Name System** or **DNS** server. To explain what DNS servers are and what they do, let's imagine that you've just started your web browser and you've typed in Google's URL, `http://www.google.com`. This address is called a **Uniform Resource Locator** or (URL) and is unique for each web site. You know that you want to use the Google search engine. But, where is the Google search engine's home page? It's obviously sitting on a server somewhere, but you've no idea where and your computer has no idea where. You computer does however know a computer who does know, either where Google's home page is, or another computer who does.

When you first turned your computer on, amongst the things it did when it started up was to ask the network for an IP address. A router on your network acting as a **Dynamic Host Configuration Protocol** (DHCP) server will have replied with an IP address for your computer and in addition the IP addresses of two DNS servers. When you typed `http://www.google.com`, knowing that it didn't know where the Google home page was, your computer constructed a packet of information with two addresses on it, the first of which was your own computer's IP address, i.e. the sender and the second, the IP address of one of the DNS servers, i.e the destination. The data inside the packet represented a request to the DNS server for the address of Google's home page server.

After a little more jiggery pokery at the router end which we need not go into here, your packet winged its way off onto the Internet and at some point a few milliseconds later got to the DNS server. The DNS server opened the packet, read your request and if it knew Google's address it created a new packet with Google's address enclosed in the data section of the packet, it put its address on the packet as sender, it used your address as the destination and sent it off back onto the Internet. If it hadn't known Google's address, it would have sent a packet to another DNS server which it hoped would know. This is repeated until a DNS server somewhere did know and returned the address to your DNS server which then returned the address to you.

In either case, a packet with Google's address in it eventually finds its way back to you.

Having got the address, your computer now constructs a new packet this time enclosing a request for the home page. It puts its address onto the packet, i.e. the sender and it adds Google's address as the destination. This packet is sent off to the router and onto the Internet, eventually to find its way across the world to Google's server. When Google's server receives the packet, it opens it, reads the request and then constructs one or possibly two or more packets with the home page code enclosed within them. It puts its address on the packets to indicate where the packets are coming from, your address to indicate where they are going to and the packets are sent back onto the Internet.

The packets arrive at your computer, they are re-assembled and displayed by the web browser. The entire activity has taken no longer than a few milliseconds.

You now know what the DNS servers do. Essentially they provide a worldwide distributed database relating URL names such as `http://www.google.com` to IP addresses because, as we have said earlier, every computer on the Internet must have a unique IP address for packets to find their to and from them. We far prefer to remember names rather than IP addresses. It's much easier to remember Google than 173.194.36.104 or Youtube rather than 209.85.229.136. Note, that if you do remember Google's IP address, you can enter 173.194.36.104 directly into your web browser, your web browser will construct a packet asking for the home page and will send it to 173.194.36.104 directly, thus bypassing the DNS servers.

A user types the address www.ocr.org.uk into a web browser. Describe how a DNS server is used to access this website and explain the advantages of using DNS servers. The quality of written communication will be assessed in your answer to this question. [A451 Jan 2012 Q4 (6)]

The examiners expected that the following points would be made.

- How DNS servers are used
  - DNS servers have a database of IP addresses
  - ...which are constantly updated by other DNS servers

- When you request an address (URL), the DNS server looks up the URL and returns the IP address, or searches for the address from other DNS servers

- Advantages
  - People do not need to remember IP addresses
  - It is easily upgradable (e.g. IPv4 to IPv6) without all web addresses needing to be the same
  - So long as you are connected to a DNS server you can have access to all the addresses

HTML

The Internet is made up of thousands of millions of computers. Every device attached to the Internet is part of it. This includes desktop computers, mobile phones, laptops, coca cola machines, (yes - there are some), jackets (amazing as it sounds, Levi and Philips have worked together to make such a jacket) and a wondrous variety of other gadgets and labour saving devices. Amongst these are hundreds of millions whose job it is to serve up web pages. These computers are running **web server** software which wait patiently on their computers for requests for web pages. When they get a packet containing a request they respond with one or more packets containing HTML code. HTML is a mnemonic for **HyperText Markup Language**. HTML was created by a British computer scientist, Tim Berners-Lee in the late 1980s and early 1990s. The first specification appeared in 1991. It described a very simple language which was intended to be used to help researchers share and refer easily to citations in electronic documents. It became clear very quickly that this could be an excellent addition to the technology of the Internet and it was taken up rapidly by researchers across the world.

Programs to read and interpret HTML were written – we call these **web browsers**. Programs to serve up documents in HTML format were created – we call these **web servers**. Programmers were employed to write documents in HTML and everything took off. Documents written in HTML were placed on servers, web browsers were used to access the servers which served up the documents which were interpreted in the browsers and displayed on screen.

In its first incarnation, HTML was a very simple language. It used a series of **tags** to signal to the web browser how to display text. An HTML file normally has extension **.html** or **.htm** and is an ordinary text file, easily readable. An example of a simple HTML file is show below.

```
<HTML>
<HEAD>
<TITLE>Sausages, bananas and apricots</TITLE>
</HEAD>

<BODY bgcolor=green>
<H1>Sausages</H1>
<P>
This picture is of some sausages ...
<IMG SRC=''http://topnews.in/health/files/Sausage121.jpg''>
<HR>
Click <A HREF=''http://www.google.com''>here</A> for a link to Google.
<P>
<H1>That's <B><I>all</I></B> folks.
</BODY>
</HTML>
```

Text enclosed between < and > are called **tags**. The tags in the example above are all written in upper case characters. This isn't necessary, it's been done here for emphasis purposes only and in fact it is good practice to write them in lower case.

The first tag <HTML> tells the web browser that the file is an HTML file. The last tag </HTML> illustrates the convention that when a tag is no longer active, a forward slash / is inserted before the tag name. In this case, </HTML> signifies that the file ends at this point.

All HTML files are made up of a HEAD and a BODY. Certain tags are expected in the HEAD, for example TITLE. The text between <TITLE> and </TITLE> will appear in the browser's title bar, in this case the text **Sausages, bananas and apricots**. The HEAD is closed by the tag </HEAD> and the BODY started. In this tag you notice that using bgcolor=green we can specify that the background colour for the page is to be green.

The next tag is <H1> which tells the browser to make the text that follows as big as possible. We need to take the tag off using </H1> otherwise all of our text that follows will also be this big. The next tag <P> instructs the browser to start a new paragraph. This tag is used extensively to make sure that we have space in between our paragraphs of text.

After the short line "This picture is about sausages ..." we introduce a new tag
`<IMG SRC=''http://topnews.in/health/files/Sausage121.jpg''>` which tells the browser to insert an image that can be found at the URL given in the tag.

The tag `<HR>` draws a horizontal ruler (line) across the screen. This is followed by another paragraph tag and then a **hyperlink** tag
`<A HREF=''http://www.google.com''>here</A>`
which highlights the word **"here"** and which when clicked will take us to the URL shown in the tag, in this case Google.

After yet another paragraph tag we have another `<H1>` tag and then `<B>` and `<I>` tags which instruct the browser to make the text between these tags, **bold** and *italic* respectively.

The body finishes with a `</BODY>` tag and the file itself finishes with `</HTML>`.

HTML as Tim Berners-Lee initially described it has become a great deal more complex as time has gone on and a working draft of the the latest version, HTML 5 was published in 2008. In addition to changes in the HTML format itself, other technologies have been created to make pages more visually appealing (video, sound, Flash animation), more dynamic (Javascript), more like printed text (Cascading Style Sheets) and more suitable of working with databases (PHP and mySQL). The budding web designer today needs to be familiar with all of these technologies if he or she is to create compelling web based content.

A rock band uses an internet website to advertise its music. The website uses HTML. Describe HTML. [A451 Jun 2011 Q3 (2)]

- HyperText Mark-up Language
- ...which is a text file containing the text to be displayed
- HTML uses tags which indicate how to display it
- ...and the location of pictures or other elements such as audio or video to include
- ...and also hyperlinks to other locations (i.e. URLs)

Explain the importance of HTML in the creation of web pages. (2)

- Web browsers are used to interpret the file and display the data correctly
- Because it is an open (i.e. accepted) standard

- ...data will display correctly on all browsers
- ...which conform to the standard

JPG, GIF, PNG, MP3 and MPEG

The World Wide Web (the web) is a very visual and auditory medium. It's pretty much impossible to imagine the web without any pictures, sound or video. How would Youtube work without video, or Flikr without pictures, or Spotify without sound?

HTML was the first language of the web and from the beginning, the web was intended to display images. These images are obviously digital, which means that they are files of large numbers of 1s and 0s which when combined into bytes, make up pixels (picture elements) that make up the image. There are various formats, or types of images. On page 76 we explained a little about JPEG, GIF and PNG files. These image formats are used universally on the web these days. JPEGs and occasionally PNG files are used for full colour images such as photographs while GIF and PNG are used for short animations and line drawings, icons and such like. All image files are inserted into an HTML web page using the `<IMG SRC='' '>` tag.

In addition to pictures, the web has become saturated with sound and video. These files are clearly different from image files and they have their own format. Sound files are typically saved as MP3, WAV, AIFF and AAC files whilst video is saved in a variety of formats, MPEG and Flash being the most common.

MP3 files are compressed audio files designed to be as small as possible whilst still retaining acceptable sound quality. MP3 files are typically ten times smaller than a normal audio file. The compression algorithm works by removing those parts of the sound that are deemed to be beyond the ability of most people to hear it. This is great for older members of the public, but your average teenager has excellent hearing and should be able to tell the difference between say a CD recording and the equivalent MP3 copy. That they rarely do so, is almost certainly due to the conditions under which most teenagers listen to MP3 files, through headphones whilst sitting on the bus or walking through a busy town complex.

WAV files are uncompressed audio files and have lost out to MP3 over recent years due to the rise in file sharing sites that have MP3 files available for download. Since they are very much smaller, MP3 files can be downloaded up to ten times quicker than the corresponding WAV file.

AIFF files are high quality audio files. They are uncompressed and are generally used in professional applications. A minute of sound in AIFF format is typically around 10 MBytes in size, considerably larger than MP3 files, though of much higher quality.

AAC files are designed to be a replacement to MP3 files. They are of higher quality for the same bit rate as MP3 files. They are found on a variety of equipment including the Apple iPhone, Sony PS3 and Sony Ericsson phones.

Video is well served on the web. MPEG from the **Moving Pictures Expert Group** is one of the most popular video formats on the web today. It has gone through various releases from MPEG-1 in 1993 to MPEG-4 in 1998. Currently under development is MPEG-V (extending MPEG to work with virtual worlds) and MPEG-U (extending MPEG to work with rich user interfaces). MPEG-4 remains a work in progress and no single software companies implements the MPEG-4 specification in all its detail. MPEG-4 was designed from the outset to work well on the Internet, where slow download speeds are common. It is a robust protocol, meaning that it has excellent error correction and it mixes video with sound and speech.

Flash video files are a very popular video format, making up the bulk of video files to be found on YouTube, Google Video, Yahoo! Video and many news providers. Flash is viewable on most operating systems using the Flash browser plug-in or the Adobe Flash Player. It is a compressed format and in some versions can be lossy, reducing colour depth when appropriate. Audio in Flash videos is usually encoded as MP3 and AAC. Despite its importance today it is possible that Flash will disappear in the relatively near future, being replaced by HTML 5 which is capable of doing everything Flash can and more.

PDF (Portable Document Format) files are open standard documents originally created by Adobe in the 1990s. Unlike many other file formats, PDF files include all of the fonts, graphics and formatting information necessary to print and display them. They are readable on pretty much every platform including PCs, Macs, tablets and smartphones. PDF files can store text and graphics in such a way that they can be printed independently of scale which makes them a common vehicle for delivering sheet music and documents which include graphics over the Internet.

ZIP is a file format used for compressing and archiving files. It was originally developed in 1989 and has since become an extremely common format for compressing material intended for download on the Internet. Algorithms to compress and decompress ZIP file formats are now built into most modern operating systems.

A list of file extensions for common file standards used on the internet is shown below.

JPG   PDF   MP3   MPEG   ZIP

A rock band's website allows some files to be downloaded by fans. Complete the table below to show which file format from the list given above may be used for each of the following files. [A451 Jun 2011 Q3 (5)]

File	File Format
A high resolution image of the band to use as a desktop background	
Sheet music of their songs ready to be printed in the correct format for guitar players	
A short video extract from their latest concert tour	
A compressed collection of 200 plain text files containing the lyrics of all their songs	
An audio recording of a song from their album	

Answer

File	File Format
A high resolution image of the band to use as a desktop background	JPG
Sheet music of their songs ready to be printed in the correct format for guitar players	PDF
A short video extract from their latest concert tour	MPEG
A compressed collection of 200 plain text files containing the lyrics of all their songs	ZIP
An audio recording of a song from their album	MP3

Importance of Compression

Compressing a file simply means reducing the size of it. There are various ways of doing this, but the overriding reason for doing so is to reduce download times. A download speed of 10 MBits per second means that we receive a MByte of data roughly every second. Compressed video and image files are typically one tenth of the size of uncompressed files. Clearly this means that they will arrive in your computer ten times faster than an uncompressed file. If you're trying to watch online video this time difference means that in the compressed case you get to watch a movie, in the uncompressed case you get to watch a series of single frames, hardly what you were hoping for.

Some file formats use compression. Explain the importance of compressing files when transmitting them via the internet. [A451 Jun 2011 Q3 (2)]

- It reduces the size of the file which needs to be transmitted
- Shortens download time
- Reduces Internet traffic (and hence probability of lost packets)
- Allows multimedia files to be streamed

Compression Algorithms

There are lossy and lossless compression algorithms. Lossy algorithms throw away some of the data in the file as part of the compression process. Clearly the idea is to throw away data that you're not going to miss and in the case of JPEG files for images and MP3 sound files, they are pretty successful since few people are able to see or hear any reduction in quality. Lossless algorithms cannot produce quite as much compression as lossy, but they retain the original quality of sound or video which is sometimes preferable. Since download speed is the paramount factor in most Internet applications, most Internet compression algorithms are lossy.

Describe the difference between lossy and lossless compression and give an example where each would be used. [A451 Jun 2011 Q3 (4)]

- In lossy compression, when the data is uncompressed it is not exactly the same as the original
- ...but the difference is so small that it cannot normally be noticed
- E.g. music files (mp3) or large resolution images for displaying on small screens.
- In lossless compression, when the data is uncompressed it is restored completely to the original file

7

Programming

Programming is the activity whereby programmers turn ideas into code. Once upon a time programmers flicked switches, up for a 0, down for 1. Each instruction to the CPU was encoded as a bank of switch positions. Once the bank of switches had been set correctly, a master switch would then be set causing the switch positions, i.e. a string of ones and zeros to be stored in the memory of the computer. The switches would then be set to the set of positions representing the next instruction and the process repeated until the entire program was committed to memory.

Today's programs are written quite differently. Programmers today write in a wide range of what are called **high level** languages such as **Visual Basic, C, C++, Pascal, Java, Perl, Python, Ruby** and a whole host of other languages, each written so as to enable a particular class of problems to be solved more easily. For example, Pascal (which first appeared in 1970) was written so as to be used specifically as a teaching language. The language is elegant, is learned easily and encourages good programming style. C++ and Java are object oriented languages which although deriving much of their structure from C (a language similar to Pascal, but much more terse) have objects at the heart of their design. The mind set of a programmer writing in C++ is quite different from that of a programmer writing in Pascal. Large programs are often written in C++ or Java.

Languages such as Perl, Python and Ruby are scripting languages, languages designed to be quick to write, relatively quick to learn and are used for tasks associated with reading and analysing data. You would tend to find them running behind the scenes in web based applications.

With so many languages available, where do you start, which one should you learn? There is no hard and fast rule and your teacher should be experienced enough to know a good starting point. We shall start however, by looking at programming in a more general way and we shall start by looking at **algo-rithms**. We have included numerous code examples in the following pages, all of which are examples taken from real code written either by us or our students.

7.1 ALGORITHMS

An algorithm is 'a sequence of steps designed to perform a particular task.'[1]

What are they?

They are recipes, the sort of things you'd use if you wanted to bake a cake (Pre-heat the oven to 180°C, prepare the base by creaming together the butter and sugar, add the flour and oats and beat them together thoroughly) or set up the Sky HD box to record a program you want to watch tomorrow (Switch the HD on, use the remote to navigate to the program selection, select date, select channel, select program and hit record).

One simple algorithm that you should be familiar with is to find the square roots of a quadratic equation. There is a (fairly) simple formula to do this. In case your memory needs refreshing, if you have a quadratic equation of the form $ax^2 + bx + c = 0$ the general solution is

$$x = \frac{-b \pm \sqrt{b^2 - 4ac}}{2a}$$

To solve a specific quadratic equation such as $x^2 - 3x - 1 = 0$ we would go through the following series of steps.

- compare $x^2 - 3x - 1 = 0$ with the general quadratic $ax^2 + bx + c = 0$, this tells us that $a = 1, b = -3$ and $c = -1$

- replace, a, b and c in the general solution formula to get

$$x = \frac{-(-3) \pm \sqrt{(-3)^2 - 4(1)(-1)}}{2(1)}$$

---

[1]A Glossary of Computing Terms, British Computing Society

i.e.

$$x = \frac{3 \pm \sqrt{9+4}}{2} = \frac{3 \pm \sqrt{13}}{2} = \frac{3 \pm 3.6056}{2}$$

(4 decimal places)

i.e.

$$x = \frac{3 + 3.6056}{2}, x = \frac{3 - 3.6056}{2}$$

so

$$x = 3.3028, x = -0.3028$$

This procedure will work for any quadratic equation where $b^2 - 4ac \geq 0$. If $b^2 - 4ac < 0$ we have no roots, simply because at this stage at least we can't find the square root of a negative number.

Problem Solving

Programmers are problem solvers. They are given a problem. They think about it. If the problem is quite big and/or complicated, they try breaking it down into smaller pieces (this is called **top-down design**). They take each of the smaller pieces and try to break them down. The intention is arrive at a set of small pieces, each of which can be turned relatively quickly and easily into code. The pieces are then re-assembled to produce the solution to the problem.

Let's consider how we might write some code to solve some simple quadratic equations.

First off, we'd need to ask the user for the coefficients of the quadratic that she wants us to solve. Next, we'd have to compare the coefficients of the general formula $ax^2 + bx + c = 0$ with the coefficients that the user has given us. We'd then check to see whether when we substitute the coefficients, we're going to get a negative number under the square root sign. To do this we'd check whether $b^2 - 4ac < 0$. If it is, we should really tell the user than there are no real roots. If $b^2 - 4ac \geq 0$ we can continue with our calculations. Finally, we need to show the user our results.

This is all very wordy. Programmers tend to avoid writing too much if they possibly can, so let's rephrase the paragraph above in two ways - firstly in what we might call **pseudo code**, i.e. english words that sort of look like, but aren't real code, useful to get our thoughts down quickly and easily and secondly in the form of a flow chart, showing how the program flows from one part to the next.

Firstly pseudo-code.

```
READ coefficients from user
IF b*b-4ac < 0
 Tell the user than there are no real roots
ELSE
 Calculate roots
 Output results
ENDIF
STOP
```

As a flowchart.

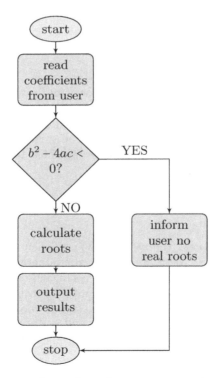

In both cases it's pretty clear what the programmer has to do. She'll need to write a routine to read the coefficients from the user, she'll have to check whether $b^2 - 4ac$ is negative, she'll have to do the actual calculation and then she'll have to say something to the user. All very straightforward.

Notice that neither the pseudo code nor the flowchart is actual code. Programmers spend much of their time writing either pseudo code or flowcharts, a combination of both or indeed any one of a hundred different ways that the programmer uses to get their thoughts down on paper. Pseudo code and flowcharts are simply two of the ways.

Frances is writing a program which simulates a dice game played with three ordinary 6-sided dice. When the player rolls the three dice, the player is given points according to the algorithm expressed in the flow diagram below.

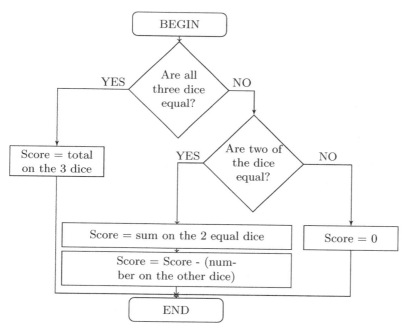

State the value of the score if the dice rolled are as follows. [A451 Jan 2011 Q11 (3)]

3 4 5

Answer : Score = 0

4 4 4

Answer : Score = 12

5 5 6

Answer : Score = 4

Some rolls of the dice result in a negative score. State a set of
three numbers which can be used to test whether the algorithm
produces a negative score when it should, and state the expected
output for your test data. (2)

All of the following will result in a negative score. One mark is given for
correct test data, the second for the correct expected score.

- 1 1 3,   expected output -1
- 1 1 4,   expected output -2
- 1 1 5,   expected output -3
- 1 1 6,   expected output -4
- 2 2 5,   expected output -1
- 2 2 6,   expected output -2

When the dice are rolled, the results are stored in an array called
DiceResult. For example, if the first dice shows a 5 then the value
of DiceResult(1) becomes 5. State the data type and size of the
array DiceResult giving a reason for each. (4)

- Data type: Integer
- Reason: A dice roll is always a whole number (between 1 and 6)
- Size: 3
- Reason : One element is needed for each dice

A mail-order company buys dresses from America and France to
sell in the UK. The company uses the following algorithm to convert sizes before printing them in its catalogue. Half sizes are not
possible (e.g. size 12.5).

```
INPUT Size
INPUT Origin
IF Origin = 'America' THEN
 Size = Size + 2
ELSE
 IF Origin = 'France' THEN
  Size = Size - 26
```

```
   END IF
END IF
PRINT Size
```

The company sells the following dresses.

Dress A	**Dress B**	**Dress C**
Origin: France	Origin: America	Origin: UK
Size: 40	Size: 8	Size: 12

State for each of the dresses, the size which will be printed in the catalogue using the algorithm given. [A451 Jan 2012 Q3 (3)]

- Dress A: 14
- Dress B: 10
- Dress C: 12

Debbie has a program on her mobile phone, which calculates the cost of the calls she has made. The algorithm to update the data when a new text call is made is shown below

```
PROCEDURE Update
    TotalCalls = TotalCalls + 1
    IF SameNetwork = TRUE THEN
        RunningCost = RunningCost + 0.01
    ELSE
        RunningCost = RunningCost + (CallLength * 0.10)
    END IF
END PROCEDURE Update
```

So far, TotalCalls = 10 and RunningCost = £12.00

Debbie makes a 3 minute call to a phone on the same network. State the values of TotalCalls and RunningCost after they have been updated using this algorithm. [A451 Specimen Paper 2012 Q4 (2)]

- TotalCalls = 11
- ... RunningCosts = £12.01

Debbie now makes a 5 minute call to a phone on a different network. State the values of TotalCalls and RunningCost after they have been updated using this algorithm. (2)

- TotalCalls = 12
- ... RunningCosts = £12.51

The examiners might ask you to produce your own pseudo code or flow diagram to solve a simple problem. In each case, take a moment to think through the problem before sketching out your solution. It's very rare for pseudo code or a flow chart to be a perfect copy of the solution first time around. There are no hard and fast rules about what constitutes pseudo code. Pseudo code is simply an attempt to describe an algorithm in English but using a code like syntax. It does not need to conform to any particular language. What is important is clarity. A well written section of pseudo code will express an algorithm clearly and succinctly and should translate into actual code without too much effort on the part of the programmer.

The following questions are examples of the sort of problems that you might be asked to solve.

The program in a vending machine uses an array called Coins to store the value in pence of all the coins that have been entered in the current sale. A maximum of 10 coins can be entered in each sale. After each sale, the array is reset so that all values are 0. Here is an example of the contents of the array Coins during a sale.

10	100	20	50	5	0	0	0	0	0

Write an algorithm to calculate the total value of the coins entered in the current sale using the contents of the array Coins. [A451 Jan 2012 Q9 (5)]

Here you are being asked to simply add up all of the elements of an array of 10 elements. This is clearly best done by writing some sort of loop. It doesn't matter which one you chose since all loops can be re-written in the form of other loops. Something that many students forget is that since we're going to produce a total we should initialise this to zero before we start otherwise we'll end up with an invalid result.

The examiners awarded marks for the following.

- Initialising the total
- (Using a loop which) correctly starts from element 1
- ... to element 10 or to the first 0 element
- ... and each element is correctly added to the total
- ... and the iterator i (or equivalent) is correctly updated in the loop.

Examples of pseudo code could be

```
i = 1
total = 0
REPEAT
 total = total + Coins(i)
 i=i+1
UNTIL i>10 or Coins(i)=0
```

or alternatively

```
total = 0
FOR i = 1 to 10
 total = total + Coins(i)
NEXT i
```

Notice that in the first pseudo code example (given by the examiners), because the last five elements of the array are zero we break out of the loop as soon as we see that we have a zero element. Clearly this wouldn't be a good idea in real code since the fact that Coins[6] is zero doesn't necessarily imply that any subsequent elements are zero. In which case we'd have left the loop before we'd have added up all the necessary elements.

The second example of pseudo code which uses a FOR loop simply adds up all the array elements after first initialising total to zero.

Note also that we assume that array indexing starts at 1 so that Coins[1] = 10 is the first element. This is not true for languages derived from C such as Java, C++ and Python where indexing starts from zero. (i.e. Coins[0] = 10 is the first element).

A dog that is 5 years old is equivalent to a 42 year old human. Ashok is writing a program which converts the age of a dog to the equivalent age for a human. The program uses the following method:

- **The user inputs age of the dog in years**
- **If the age is 2 or less, the human equivalent is 12 times the age**
- **If the age is more than 2, the human equivalent is 24 for the first 2 years, plus 6 for every additional year.**

Write an algorithm to calculate and output the human equivalent of the age of a dog using the method described. [A451 Jun 2011 Q9 (5)]

The examiners awarded marks for an algorithm that ...

- Allows real age to be input
- If age <= 2
    - multiply real age by 12
- Else If age > 2
    - Work out extra years (i.e. real age 2)
    - ... multiply by 6
    - ... and add 24 (for the first 2 years)

The examiners also provided an example in pseudo-code form.

```
BEGIN
 Input RealAge
 IF RealAge <= 2
  DogYears = RealAge * 12
 ELSE
  ExtraYears = RealAge - 2
  DogYears = 24 + ExtraYears * 6
 END IF
END
```

A display board can show a flashing message of up to 20 characters.

Write an algorithm for the program which:

- **Allows the user to input the message and the number of flashes**
- **Rejects the message if it is longer than 20 characters and stops**
- **Otherwise it repeatedly displays the message and clears the display for the correct number of times.** [A451 Specimen Paper 2010 Q12 (5)]

The examiners suggested the following pseudo code algorithm. Note the `Wait` statements after displaying and clearing the message. The first is essential otherwise the message would be instantly cleared once it had been displayed.

```
Begin
 Input Message
 Input NumberOfFlashes
 If length(Message) > 20 Then
```

```
   Output 'This message is too long'
  Else
   For i = 1 to NumberOfFlashes
    Display Message
    Wait
    Clear Message
    Wait
   Next
  End If
End
```

Clearly it is likely that the algorithm written by many if not most students will differ from this. This doesn't matter. The examiners awarded marks for an algorithm which:

- Inputs a message and number of flashes
- If length of message > 20, outputs an error message and stops
- Otherwise it runs a loop which will
- ...flash the message
- ...for the correct number of times

7.2   PROGRAMMING LANGUAGES

Once the programmer has jotted down his thoughts and algorithms down on paper it's time to turn these into code. Code can't be written in English or indeed any other human language for one very good reason. Human languages are ambiguous, which means that any given sentence may have more than one interpretation. This is great for writing poetry and prose, but no good at all for a computer. Take for example the sentence, **"fruit flies like a banana"**. Do we mean that fruit flies like eating bananas or that fruit (of any fashion, could be an apple, an orange, kiwi fruit etc) when thrown, flies through the air in much the same way as does a banana? This is a classic example of ambiguity in English and clearly we can't allow such sentences to be constructed if we want to program computers. So, we have to create artificial languages in which such sentences cannot be written.

High Level or Low Level?

Over the seventy years or so since the first computer (ENIAC - short for **"Electronic Numerical Integrator and Computer"**, first commissioned in July 1946) thousands of computer languages have been created. Most of these were obscure offerings, only used by a small number of people and now probably defunct, others have become the programming language of choice

for thousands of programmers world wide. Popular languages would include
C[2], **C++**[3], **Pascal**[4], **Java**[5], **Visual Basic**[6] and **Python**[7].

All of the above are examples of **high-level** languages. This essentially
means that the syntax of the language, i.e. the structure of the language is
relatively close to English, but without the ambiguities inherent in English.
To show you what we mean, let's suppose that we want to print the numbers
1 to 10, their squares and their cubes in Pascal and in C.

```
Code snippet in Pascal
i : integer;

for i:=1 to 10 do
begin
  println (i, i*i, i*i*i);
end;


Code snippet in C
int i;

for (i=1; i<=10; i++)
{
  printf (``\%d, \%d, \%d'', i, i*i, i*i*i);
}
```

It's pretty easy to see what both of these snippets of code are doing. Both
are using a FOR loop. The syntax is different, but they're pretty similar.
Both languages need you to **declare** a variable before you use it. Some languages don't need you to do this, but Pascal, C and its derivatives do. In
both cases we're going to use a variable i and in both cases we want i to be
an integer. For those of you unfamiliar with maths, an integer is any whole
number positive or negative and including zero. So, for example, 4,213 is an

---

[2]a general-purpose computer programming language developed between 1969 and 1973
by Dennis Ritchie at the Bell Telephone Laboratories for use with the Unix operating
system

[3]a successor to C created by Bjarne Stroustrup in 1979. It extends C by adding classes,
operator overloading and a number of other useful constructs

[4]published in 1970 by Niklaus Wirth as a small and efficient language intended to en-
courage good programming practices using structured programming and data structuring

[5]developed by James Gosling at Sun Microsystems. The language derives much of its
syntax from C and C++ but has a simpler object model and fewer low-level facilities

[6]a Microsoft product, derived from BASIC, it enables the rapid application development of graphical user interface applications

[7]a general purpose language created by Guido van Rossum in 1989

integer as is -27 and 0.

We then use this integer as a counter to count from 1 to 10 in each case printing out the value of i, the value of i^2 and the value of i^3. Pascal uses **begin** and **end** to delimit the block of code that the for loop is operating on, C uses { and }. Otherwise the syntax is very similar.

Take a look at the following example of code written in Visual Basic.

```
Module QuickTest

    Sub Main()
        Dim strIngInput As String

        Console.WriteLine("Enter 'q' to quit..., otherwise please type something")
        Do
            strIngInput = Console.ReadLine()
            Console.WriteLine("You typed " & strIngInput)
            Console.WriteLine("Again?, remember 'q' to quit")
        Loop While (strIngInput <> "q")
        Console.WriteLine("Finished now.")
    End Sub

End Module
```

Can you work out what it does?

It starts off by declaring that **stringInput** has the datatype **String** and then goes on to ask the user for some input, echoes it on the screen and continues to do so until the user presses 'q' when the program ends.

So far we have seen examples of high level languages. In contrast, a snippet of code from a low-level language, often called assembly language, that will run on Intel processors is shown below.

```
PGROUP        Group        PROG
DGROUP        Group        DATA

DATA Segment Public 'DATA'
 public brkflag
 brkflag DW        0
DATA ends
```

```
PROG Segment Para Public 'PROG'
 public TrapBrea
 assume cs:PGROUP,DS:DGROUP

TrapBrea proc near
        push ds
        push cs
        pop ds
        mov dx,offset PGROUP:Bret
        mov ah,25h
        mov al,23h
        int 21h
        pop ds
        ret
TrapBrea endp

PROG ends
        end
```

This is quite different to the previous examples. Unless you know the instruction set on this particular microprocessor, in this case an Intel processor, you really wouldn't have much idea what is going on. The examiners want you to appreciate the difference between high and low level languages but there is no requirement to become proficient in a low level language. The assumption is that you will start your programming career in Visual Basic, or perhaps Pascal, Java or one of the high level scripting languages such as Javascript or Python. Very few computer scientists today are proficient in low level languages, which is a shame because such proficiency gives you absolute mastery over computer hardware. Low-level languages are called low-level because they are very, very close to the actual binary code running on the CPU. Each line of the code above inside the procedure **TrapBrea** are CPU instructions that operate directly on the registers of the CPU.

All low level languages look something like this. To program effectively in assembly language, programmers need to understand how the microprocessor works, what its instruction set is and how quickly each instruction can execute. Admittedly, it might take tens or hundreds of lines of code in assembly language to duplicate the functionality provided by a handful of lines in a high-level language, but sometimes there is no other way of getting the CPU to do precisely what you want. In the case of some devices, for example washing machines or car management systems, there are invariably no high level languages that will run on them.

Note that each distinct microprocessor has its own particular assembly language. The assembly language written for an Intel microprocessor will be quite different from a microprocessor from Motorola or Hitachi for example.

Translators

Having written our algorithms in one of the high or low-level languages what happens next? Well, you know that CPUs only understand binary, and if we've just written something in Visual Basic or Java, that's hardly binary. We need a translator. In exactly the same way that you'd need an translator if you went to some obscure part of the Amazon jungle on holiday, we need a translator to convert what we've written in our high-level language into the binary code (often called **machine code**) that the CPU needs. Although low-level languages are closer to to binary than high-level, they also need translating, though in this case the translator has a much easier job to do.

Explain why a program written in a high level language needs to be translated before it can be executed. [A451 Specimen Paper 2012 Q10 (3)]

- A high level language (HLL) is understood by humans
- However, computers, i.e. the CPU can only execute machine code instructions and doesn't understand high level languages
- So we need a translator to convert a program in a HLL to an equivalent program in machine code

Assemblers, Compilers and Interpreters

There are essentially three different types of translator. If you've written your program in a low-level language, usually called an assembly language, you'll need an **assembler** to convert to binary code. Each different microprocessor has its own unique instruction set which means that each different microprocessor has its own assembler program.

If you've written your program in a high-level language there are two types of translator you would use. A **compiler** takes the program you have written and translates it in its entirety into binary code. For a short program this is pretty much instantaneous. For a larger program with the **source code**, i.e. the code that you have written, split across many files, this might take from a few minutes to some hours. The resulting program (after a process called **linking** in which your code is linked with any library code it needs) can then run on any computer with the same processor and running the same operating system as yours. The advantages of a compiler is that the final code will run quickly on the target machine and in the commercial world, since the final program is in binary code it is difficult though not totally impossible to work out the source code. Its disadvantage is that the development process itself is quite slow, with the typical **edit, compile, run** cycle taking some time.

An **interpreter** on the other hand is a translator that reads each line of your code, translates it into binary and then runs it immediately. This is great for development, because it is quick and easy to write and test, but because it takes time to read, translate and run for every line, the program itself is not going to run quickly. In addition, in the commercial world, its not a good idea to give away your source code, and if your program is only ever interpreted, you'd need to release the source code to the purchaser.

A compiler and an interpreter are two different types of translator. Describe one difference between a compiler and an interpreter.
[A451 Specimen Paper 2012 Q10 (2)]

- A compiler translates the entire program before execution
- . . . whereas an interpreter translates and executes one line at a time before moving on to the next line and repeating the process
- A compiler creates a list of errors after compilation
- . . . whereas an interpreter stops after the first error
- A compiler produces an independent executable file
- . . . whereas an interpreted program needs the interpreter each time it is run
- A compiled program is translated once
- . . . whereas an interpreted program is translated each time it is run

Common Programming Tools

How does the programmer make sure that his program works correctly? He (or quite commonly she) will do her level best to make sure during the design process that the algorithms are correct. She'll do this by **dry running** it, i.e. going through the code carefully line by line to try to make sure that every line is correct. A good editing program will help with **syntax highlighting**, whereby reserved words in the language such as **if, for, then, int** etc. are shown in different colours. If she's a good programmer she will **annotate** the code, i.e. put comments throughout the code explaining what various lines of the code do. She will **indent** the code so that blocks of code inside control loops are clearly associated with the loop structure, (more on this later) and she will choose sensible variable names so that for example in a program that calculates the VAT on an item she'll write a line such as

```
float VAT = 0.20;
productPrice = originalPrice + originalPrice * VAT;
```

rather than

```
float v = 0.20;
pp = op * v;
```

The compiler will help her a great deal by highlighting syntactical errors. For example in languages like C, C++ and Java it's necessary to put a semi-colon at the end of many (but not all) of the lines. The compiler will throw up an error if a line needs it and the programmer hasn't written it. Similarly, if when writing in Pascal, the programmer writes `printline` when she should really have written `println` the compiler will tell her.

Modern programming development environments are called **IDEs** or **Integrated Development Environments**. These have an editor, a compiler, a linker and a button or a menu item that will allow the programmer to run the resulting program without stepping outside of the environment. This allows the programmer to write, test and **debug** the program quickly and relatively easily. Testing and debugging, i.e. finding the bugs in a program, can be a very tedious, long winded process. With the best will in the world, even if you are one of the world's best programmers, you will inevitably write code that has bugs in it. It really is pretty impossible to find all of the bugs in a program because in large programs there are effectively an infinite number of paths through the program, so it is inconceivable to test all of them. The best that a programmer can hope to do is to test routes through the program that are most likely to be used.

With most modern IDEs it is possible to do **source level debugging**. This is where the programmer is able to **step** through his code line by line watching the variables change as he goes. He is able to set **breakpoints**. These are markers placed on lines in the code that cause the program to pause when the program is about to execute the marked line. When the program reaches the line and pauses, the programmer can check the values of all of her variables, making sure that they are as she would expect. Using the **debugger** in this way will help the programmer find even the most subtle bug.

Another tool that programmers find very useful is an **automated documentation** tool. This is used in the following way. For each function and
section of code that the programmer writes, she places comments explaining
what the function or section is intended to do. These comments are preceded
by special characters such as $ or % signs. When the programmer wants to
produce a summary of the code, but without the code itself she can run the
automated document tool on the source code. The tool will read the source
code searching for the special characters and pulling out the comments associated with them. The comments are appended to a file of such comments
and can be used by the programmer as a reference document for the project.

Finally, on more sophisticated projects and/or when working as a member
of a team where perhaps three or four of you are working on the same set
of source files the source files can be held in a **source repository**. When
a programmer wants to work on a particular source file, she will **check out**
the file, locking it so that no-one else can access it whilst she has it. When
she has finished editing the file she can **check in** the file, putting it back
into the source repository. This unlocks it, allowing other members of the
team to work on it. If at any time the source files reach a critical point, a
snapshot can be taken of the source files, stored in the repository and when,
maybe weeks later after many edits of each of the source files, it is necessary
to go back to the earlier critical point, perhaps because further work has introduced numerous errors, the snapshot can be released from the repository
and work can restart on the files from the snapshot.

**Describe tools and facilities available in an integrated development
environment (IDE) which can help the programmer to identify and
correct syntax errors.** [A451 Jan 2011 Q8 (4)]

- Error messages and diagnostics are produced
- . . . when code is translated by the compiler
- . . . or on the fly while writing code by the interpreter
- Both will attempt to tell you what the error is
- . . . and indicate where the it is giving the line number or underlining
  the error
- The editor
- . . . allows you to enter the corrected code

7.3   CONTROL FLOW

On page 132, we showed a flowchart of how we might work out the possible
values of x in a quadratic equation. Flow charts are very good at showing

how a program flows from one thing to the next, hence the name. At one point we had to make a decision as to whether we could find values for x at all. If $b^2 - 4ac < 0$, this meant that we'd have to try to find the square root of a negative number, and at GCSE this simply isn't possible. If this had occurred, we'd simply have to tell the user that we couldn't find any values for x and we'd have to stop. If it hadn't, we could calculate the two possible values of x before stopping.

Sequence

Much of the time code is executed in **sequence**. I.e. one line is executed, then the next line down is executed, then the next and so on. However, on occasion as in the example above we need to make a decision.

Selection

This is called making a **selection**. In the quadratic example based on the result of calculating the value of $b^2 - 4ac$ we'd select to go down one route and giving the user an error message if the result was negative, calculating values for x if the result was zero or positive. A typical piece of code in Java might be something along the following lines.

```
void show ()
{
  if (newBallNeeded)  // we need a new ball
  {
    // create a new one
    ball = new ball ((int)(width/2), (int)(height/2));
    newBallNeeded = false;
  }
  else
  {
    checkForCollisions ();

    // re-calculate and redraw our ball
    ball.recalculate();
    ball.redraw();
  }
} // show
```

The code is taken from a game called **breakout** written to mimic the classic video game released by Atari in 1976. In the function **show()**, we first check to see whether we need a new ball. If we do, we create one, if not, we check for collisions, re-calculate the position of the ball based upon its velocity in both the x and y directions and then redraw it.

Another example, again written in Java, this time to translate a given string into Morse code is given below. This example makes use of two forms of selection, **if** and **case**

```
void updateBeacon ()
{
  if (weHaveAMorseString)
  { // if we've reached the end of the string, reset our pointers
    if (morseStringPtr == morseString.length())
    {
      morseStringPtr = 0;
      weHaveAMorseString = false;
    }
    else // we're still parsing our string
    {
      switch (morseString.charAt (morseStringPtr))
      {
        case '.':
          morseDelay = dots;
          break;
        case '-':
          morseDelay = dash;
          break;
        case '$':
          morseDelay = intraLetterSpace;
          break;
      }
      morseStringPtr += 1;
    }
  }
  else
    ... some other code
} // void updateBeacon
```

Here we have what is called a **nested IF** statement, i.e. one if statement inside another plus a case statement. Case statements are a shorter way of writing a series of **IF...ELSE** statements. The code above could have been re-written as

```
char c = morseString.charAt (morseStringPtr);
if (c == '.') then
{
  morseDelay = dots;
}
```

```
else if (c=='-')
{
  morseDelay = dash;
}
else if (c=='$')
{
  morseDelay = intraLetterSpace;
}
```

Which do you think looks more elegant?

Iteration

The **for** loops on page 140 are an example of **iteration**. Each programming language has its own syntax for iterating, i.e. repeating something. FOR loops are fairly universal, but there are others. The Visual Basic example on page 141 uses a DO...LOOP WHILE construct to allow the user to keep entering text until they enter a letter 'q' for quit.

The following is an example of a REPEAT...UNTIL loop.

```
i := 0;
repeat
  i := i+1;
  ... some code
until (i > 10);
```

In this example, the code inside the REPEAT... UNTIL block is executed until the condition after the until is met. In this case until (i > 10) is true.

The important thing to ask about each of these iteration constructs is, at what point do they terminate? FOR loops run for a fixed number of iterations. REPEAT...UNTIL loops run at least once because the condition under which they terminate is not checked until the end. WHILE loops on the other hand check the termination condition at the beginning of the loop, so the code may not run at all.

Frances is writing a program which simulates a dice game played with three ordinary 6-sided dice. When the dice are rolled, the results are stored in an array called DiceResult. The routine for rolling the dice is written as a sequence below.

```
BEGIN RollTheDice
  DiceResult(1) = Random Number between 1 and 6
  DiceResult(2) = Random Number between 1 and 6
```

```
DiceResult(3) = Random Number between 1 and 6
END
```

Rewrite this routine so that it uses iteration. You may use a diagram. [A451 Jan 2011 Q11 (4)]

The examiners awarded marks for code or a diagram that illustrated the following points.

- Using a loop
- i (or equivalent) initialised correctly
- Correct end condition for loop/loops the required number of times
- Correct use of i (or equivalent) in DiceRoll(i)

The examiners provided an example of the sort of code that might be written.

```
BEGIN RollTheDice
  i=1
  WHILE i <= 3
    DiceRoll(i) = Random Number between 1 and 6
    i=i+1
  END WHILE
END
```

An alternative using a FOR loop might be written as ...

```
BEGIN RollTheDice
  FOR i=1 To 3
    DiceRoll(i) = Random Number between 1 and 6
  END FOR
END
```

Or, as a REPEAT...UNTIL loop ...

```
BEGIN RollTheDice
  i=1
  REPEAT
    DiceRoll(i) = Random Number between 1 and 6
    i=i+1
  UNTIL i>3
END
```

7.4   Data Handling

All programs operate on data. What is data? If you cast your minds back to the chapter on databases on page 87, data is **"information coded and** structured for subsequent processing, generally by a computer system."[8]. Note, data is plural, datum is singular. We should really say 'data are' rather than 'data is', but 'data is' is so prevalent that it's not worth getting into an argument over it.

OK, so what does that actually mean as far as programmers are concerned?

Variables and Constants

At some point in your program you're going to have to store stuff. For example, if we're trying to solve the general quadratic equation $ax^2 + bx + c = 0$, when we ask our user to tell us what the values of a, b and c are, we're going to have to keep track of them somehow. In most cases at GCSE, a, b and c are going to be whole numbers, i.e. integers, but it's perfectly possible that our user might want us to solve an equation like $2.1x^2 - 3.2x + 4.75 = 0$. In this case a, b and c are not whole numbers, but what programmers call floating point or real numbers. We keep track by storing them in **variables** that we create especially for them.

The 'official' definition of a variable is **"the identifier (or name) associated with a particular memory location used to store data"**[9].

In the case of our quadratic equation we're going to need at least three variables, which it makes sense to call a, b and c. Shall our variables store integers or shall we store floats? Note that in most (but not all) languages, once you create a variable to store an integer, you can't change your mind later and try to store a float in it. The compiler will complain. If we want to cope with anything our user may throw at us, it's probably better to set up our variables as floats not integers because floats can store integers, but integers can't store floats.

In many languages, including C, C++, Java and Pascal, variables need to be **declared** before they are used. In the case of our quadratic this would simply be a case of writing (in C, C++ or Java)

```
float a, b, c;
```

At some point we'd need to **initialise** our variables by actually setting them equal to something by writing

---

[8]British Computing Society, A Glossary of Computing Terms
[9]British Computing Society, A Glossary of Computing Terms

```
c = 4.2;
```

Often, we declare and initialise in one line such as

```
float c = 4.2;
```

If we're writing a program that uses values that don't change, for example the number of legs on a donkey (usually 4) or more commonly $\pi = 3.14159265$ (to 8 decimal places), in Pascal we could use

```
const pi = 3.14159265;
```

The fundamental difference between constants and variables is that while you can change the contents of a variable during the program if you try to do the same with something that you have declared is constant later, the compiler will complain and refuse to compile your program for you. So, for example you can do this

```
float c = 4.2;
c = 2.176;
```

but you cannot do this

```
const numberOfLegsOnDonkey = 4;
numberOfLegsOnDonkey = 3;
```

A program contains the following code to calculate the circumference of a bicycle wheel, using the wheel size (diameter).

```
BEGIN
 CONSTANT Pi = 3.14
 INPUT WheelSize
 Circumference = Pi * WheelSize
 OUTPUT Circumference
END
```

The code uses one constant and two variables. State the names of the constant and the variables. [A451 Jun 2011 Q7 (2)]

- Constant: Pi
- Variables: WheelSize, Circumference

Explain one difference between a constant and a variable. (2)

- The value of a constant is set when the constant is declared
- The value of a variable is set while the program is running
- The value of a constant cannot be changed once the program is running, i.e. can only be set at design time

- A variable has no value at design time

A program includes the following code.

```
01 If A > B Then
02   A = B
03   B = A
04 End If
```

The code uses the variables A and B. Describe what is meant by a variable. [A451 Specimen Paper 2010 Q8 (2)]

- A name
- ... which is used to identify a (memory) location
- ... used to store a value which can change

Which Data Types

Which data types do you use in your program and when? Take a look at the following program in Pascal which solves our little quadratic problem for us.

Numbers and Booleans

```
program quadratic;

var
  a, b, c, determinant, x1, x2 : real;

begin
  writeln ('Running quad');
  write ('Enter a: ');
  readln (a);
  write ('Enter b: ');
  readln (b);
  write ('Enter c: ');
  readln (c);

  determinant := b*b - 4 * a * c;
  if (determinant < 0) then
    writeln ('No real roots')
  else
  begin
    x1 := (-b + sqrt(determinant)) / (2*a);
    x2 := (-b - sqrt(determinant)) / (2*a);
    writeln ('Two roots : ', x1:4:2, ' and ', x2:4:2);
```

```
   end;
end.
```

In this code, we've used six variables, all real numbers. a, b and c are used to store the values that the user gives us. *determinant* is used to store the value of the calculation of $b^2 - 4ac$. $x1$ and $x2$ hold the roots.

In the next (artificial) example we'll use a boolean and char datatype. We'll use the boolean variable **leave** to tell us when to quit. We set **leave** to be false at the beginning. We go into a repeat loop and stay there until the user types the letter 'q' in which case we set **leave** to be true so that when we reach the 'until' part of the loop we will exit the loop. The variable c is of datatype **char**, and its job is to hold the letter that the user types. The function **readln** simply reads the keyboard with the key that the user types being put into the variable c.

```
program exampleBoolean;
var
    leave : boolean;
      c    : char;

begin
  leave := false;
  repeat
    write('Type 'q' to quit:');
    readln(a);
    if c = 'q' then
      leave := true
  until leave = true;
end.
```

A program includes the following code.

```
01 If A > B Then
02   A = B
03   B = A
04 End If
```

State the final values of the variables A and B if the values at the beginning of the code are
    A = 4 B = 9 [A451 Specimen Paper 2010 Q8 (1)]

Answer:

- Final value of A = 4

- Final value of B = 9

If A = 6 B = 2 (1)

Answer:

- Final value of A = 2
- Final value of B = 2

The intention of lines 02 and 03 is to swap the contents of the variables A and B. This does not work. Rewrite the code so that the contents of the variables are swapped correctly. (3)

Clearly we need to save one of the variables someplace else otherwise as in the code above, we lose the contents of A, so one possible solution could be

```
01 If  A > B  Then
02    temporaryVariable = A
03    A = B
04    B = temporaryVariable
05 End If
```

The examiners awarded marks for:

- The contents of one variable are stored in a temporary variable
- So that the second variable can be copied into the first
- Then the temporary variable can be used to update the second variable

The examiners will want to know that you understand a range of datatypes. **Integers** hold whole numbers like 56, -127 and 0. **Reals**, also called **floats** in some languages are used to store numbers with decimal points like 3.14159, -267.7891 and 2.236. **Booleans** are variables that are either true or false. **Chars** hold single characters like the letters 'A' or '@' and **Strings** store a collection of alphanumeric characters such as the sentence 'Fruit flies like a banana'.

A program uses two variables, WheelSize which is an integer and Circumference which is real number. Explain the difference between an integer and a real number. [A451 Jun 2011 Q7 (2)]

- An integer is a whole number
- A real number can include decimal fractions

A display board can show a flashing message of up to **20** characters.

A program allows users to input the message to be displayed and the number of times it should flash. State the data type of each item of the input data. [A451 Specimen Paper 2010 Q12 (1,1)]

- Message: String
- Number of flashes: Integer

A mail-order company buys dresses from America and France to sell in the UK. The company uses the following algorithm to convert sizes before printing them in its catalogue. Half sizes are not possible (e.g. size **12.5**).

```
INPUT Size
INPUT Origin
IF Origin = 'America' THEN
  Size = Size + 2
ELSE
  IF Origin = 'France' THEN
    Size = Size - 26
  END IF
END IF
PRINT Size
```

The code uses the variables Origin and Size. Describe what is meant by a variable. [A451 Jan 2012 Q3 (2)]

- A name/symbol which represents a value in a program
- ...which points to a memory location
- ...and whose value be changed while the program is running

State the most appropriate data type for the variables Origin and Size, giving a reason for your choice. (4)

Origin

- Data type: String
- Reason: Consists of characters

Size

- Data type: Integer
- Reason: Consists of whole numbers

Debbie has a program on her mobile phone, which calculates the cost of the calls she has made. The program uses the following variables. State the most appropriate data type for each variable. [A451 Specimen Paper 2012 Q4 (5)]

Variable name	Purpose	Data type
Network	The name of the mobile phone network operator used (e.g. Toki Weka)	
CallLength	The length of a call made. (e.g. 1.5 for one and a half minutes)	
SameNetwork	Whether a call was made to a phone on the same network	
TotalCalls	The total number of calls made (e.g. 10)	
RunningCost	The calculated cost of all calls (e.g. £12.00)	

Answer:

Variable name	Purpose	Data type
Network	The name of the mobile phone network operator used (e.g. Toki Weka)	string/text/alphanumeric
CallLength	The length of a call made. (e.g. 1.5 for one and a half minutes)	real/float/single/double
SameNetwork	Whether a call was made to a phone on the same network	boolean
TotalCalls	The total number of calls made (e.g. 10)	integer
RunningCost	The calculated cost of all calls (e.g. £12.00)	currency/real

One Dimensional Arrays

In the program to calculate the quadratic equation, we used **readln** three times to read numbers into three variables a, b and c each of which would hold a real number. We wanted three numbers, so we used three variables. Let's suppose for a moment that we wanted to read 100 numbers instead. Does this mean we need a hundred variables too? Well, actually yes we do.

But this is a problem since with only 26 letters in the english alphabet, we'll quickly run out of variables. So, perhaps we should use a combination of letters and numbers like a1, a2, a3, ..., a100 for example. That would work, but do we really want to write out code like the following ...

```
   a1, a2, a3, a4, a5 : real;
   a6, a7, a8, a9, a10 : real;
{all the way to}
   a96, a97, a98, a99, a100 : real;
{and then we need readln for each of these - far, far too long!}
```

There is a better way. We can use something called a one-dimensional array. In Pascal you declare a one dimensional array like this

```
   a : array[1..100] of real;
```

This line creates a list of 100 real numbers all of which are called a. The first **element** or **member** of the array is a[1], the second is a[2], the third is a[3] and so on up to the last element, a[100]. If we store our 100 real numbers in an array, we can write a FOR loop to ask the user for 100 reals like this.

```
   a : array[1..100] of real;
   counter : integer;

   for counter := 1 to 100 do
   begin
     readln(a[counter]);
   end;
```

This code has declared two variables, a one-dimensional array called a which can store 100 real numbers and an integer called counter. counter counts up from 1 to 100, on each occasion reading a real number from the keyboard and storing it in a, using the counter as an **index** into the array. The first time through the loop, counter = 1, so we store our incoming real number into a[1].

counter hasn't reached 100 yet so it runs through the loop a second time, this time counter = 2 and we store our new incoming real number in a[2]. This continues all the way up to a[100].

Arrays are really useful data structures. They are a very compact way of storing large amounts of data. To use them you need to give them a name, state what datatype they can store and how big they are, i.e. how many data items they can store.

Note that in Pascal and in VisualBasic the first element of an array `myArray`
with n elements is `myArray[1]` and the last element is `myArray[n]`. In many
other languages such as C, Java and Python, array elements start at 0 so
that the first element of an array `myArray` would be `myArray[0]` and the last
element would be `myArray[n-1]`.

**The program in a vending machine uses an array called Coins to
store the value in pence of all the coins that have been entered in
the current sale. A maximum of 10 coins can be entered in each
sale. After each sale, the array is reset so that all values are 0.
Here is an example of the contents of the array Coins during a
sale.**

10	100	20	50	5	0	0	0	0	0

**In the example above, the value of Coins(1) is 10. State the value
of Coins(4) and Coins(10)** [A451 Jan 2012 Q9 (2)]

- Coins(4) = 50
- Coins(10) = 0

Describe what is meant by an array. [A451 Jan 2011 Q11 (2)]

- A data structure or a collection of several variables
- . . . under one name
- Each individual variable is given an index
- . . . by which it is referred within the array

**Zak is writing a program that uses an array called WordList. This
array contains 10 foreign words in alphabetical order. The contents
of the array are shown below.**

Wordlist(1)	akesi
Wordlist(2)	esun
Wordlist(3)	jaki
Wordlist(4)	kala
Wordlist(5)	lipu
Wordlist(6)	mama
Wordlist(7)	nasa
Wordlist(8)	olin
Wordlist(9)	taso
Wordlist(10)	walo

The value of Wordlist(1) is "akesi". Complete the following statements.

The value of Wordlist(6) is . . .
The value of Wordlist(. . .) is "taso" [A451 Specimen Paper 2012 Q11 (2)]

Answers:

- The value of Wordlist(6) is "mama"
- The value of Wordlist(9) is "taso"

Zak needs to write a routine that:

- allows the user to input a word
- goes through the items in the array WordList in turn, starting from the WordList(1)
- if it finds the word that the user has input, it outputs "Word found".

Write an algorithm for this routine in pseudocode. (5)

The following example code is provided by the examiners, but you are not expected to have produced code exactly the same as this.

```
INPUT SearchWord
I=0
REPEAT
 I=I+1
 IF WordList(I) = SearchWord THEN
    OUTPUT ''Word Found''
 END IF
UNTIL I = 10
```

Alternatively, this could be written using a simple FOR loop such as the following.

```
INPUT SearchWord
FOR I = 1 TO 10
 IF WordList(I) = SearchWord THEN
    OUTPUT ''Word Found''
 END IF
```

The examiners allocated marks in the following way where each bullet point is worth 1 mark up to a total of 5.

- Input a word

- Code contains a loop starting from item 1
- ...compares the word searched to the current item
- ...outputs Word Found if there is a match
- Loop stops when you get to item 10
- ...or when the item has been found
- ...or when the current word is higher in alphabet than the searchword.

7.5 TESTING

We've written our code, we've checked and re-checked it and we're sure that it's all going to work. How are we sure? What have we done to make sure that it works?

Syntax and Logic Errors

The first check on our code is done by the compiler (or perhaps our interpreter if that's our translator). Any **syntax errors** should have been picked up at that point. What is a syntax error? It's an error where what we wrote hasn't complied with the rules of the language that we're writing in. For example, if you're writing in Pascal, most, but not all statements need to end in a semi-colon (i.e. a ';'). If we put a semi-colon where we shouldn't have, or more likely, we didn't when we should have, our translator will complain and hopefully tell us exactly where we made the mistake. Similarly, if we want to print something to the screen, we'd need to write **println** in Pascal and **print** in Visual Basic. If we'd written something else such as **printline** in Pascal, the translator will complain.

There are other types of errors in our code that won't get picked up by the translator. Suppose our program was meant to check that $b^2 - 4ac < 0$ but we checked that $b^2 - 4ac \leq 0$ instead. In the case where $b^2 - 4ac = 0$ we'd report that there were no real roots, which would be wrong. There are real roots, it so happens that there is a single repeated root. This is an example of a **logic error**. Logic errors aren't picked up until the program runs.

Similarly, what would happen if the user entered 0 for a in the quadratic program? The program calculates roots according to the formula

$$x = \frac{-b \pm \sqrt{b^2 - 4ac}}{2a}$$

If $a = 0$ we'd end up dividing by zero and you probably know that you can't divide anything by zero. In the case of the computer, the program would

simply crash. Computers simply can't divide by zero. This is known as a
runtime error.

The program in a vending machine uses an array called Coins to
store the value in pence of all the coins that have been entered in
the current sale. A maximum of 10 coins can be entered in each
sale. After each sale, the array is reset so that all values are 0.
Here is an example of the contents of the array Coins during a
sale.

10	100	20	50	5	0	0	0	0	0

An algorithm to reset the contents of the array Coins after each
sale is shown below. This algorithm contains a logic error.

```
i=1
REPEAT
 Coins(i) = 0
 i=i+1
UNTIL i = 10
```

State what is meant by a logic error. [A451 Jan 2012 Q9 (1)]

- The program is written to do something other than what the programmer intended

Explain why the algorithm above contains a logic error. (2)

- It will only reset the first 9 elements and will not reset the 10th element
- After setting Coins(9) = 0, i will become10
- ...and the loop will stop
- The final line should say UNTIL i > 10

**A syntax error can occur when writing a program. State what is
meant by a syntax error, giving an example.** [A451 Jan 2011 Q8 (2)]

- An error in the rules/grammar of the language
- Any suitable example will get the second mark, for example a spelling
  error such as PRITN instead of PRINT

**Vimal is writing a program to convert the time from the 24 hour
clock to the 12 hour clock. Here is an extract from his program.
This extract contains two errors.**

```
IF (hours > 12) ADN (hours < 24) THEN
    hours = hours + 12
END IF
```

Explain why there is an error in the first line, and state what type of error this is. [A451 Specimen Paper 2012 Q8 (3)]

- The keyword AND has been misspelled
- The symbol ADN will not be recognised
- This breaks the rules of the language
- Type of error: syntax error

Explain why there is an error in the second line, and state what type of error this is. (3)

- It is adding instead of subtracting
- It will produce the wrong result because the answer will be bigger than 24
- Type of error: logic error

Test Data

How do we find these errors before the user does? By reading the code lots of times? Or can we test the program beforehand? What does that mean? How do we **test** code?

Testing is a fundamental part of programming. Highly experienced programmers often start a new project by writing test code first, before any actual code to solve the problem has been written. By thinking about how you might test something before you actually start writing it, you'll have a very clear idea of what the program should do. Most programmers do it the other way around. They think of a solution to a problem, they create a suitable algorithm, they write the code in their favourite language and then they test it. At which point, their test procedures are designed with their solution in mind. This isn't such a good idea and is why the programmers who wrote the code are invariably the worst at testing their own code.

Programmers get very protective about their code and will almost never test it properly in case it breaks the code. Nobody wants to see their programs crash, so programmers will rarely test their code thoroughly even though they believe they are doing so. Colleagues on the other hand will happily try to get the program to crash as quickly as possible, and they will usually succeed.

So what is good testing?

Good testing is anticipating what the user is likely to try and do with the program and to write code that copes with whatever the user does. It means trying to cover all possible pathways through the program. For example, in our small program to solve a quadratic equation what would happen if when the user was asked for the coefficient of x^2, i.e. a, the user typed in a negative number? Would it still work? Yes it would.

Would it still work if the user entered a letter 'a' for example?

In this case it wouldn't work. The program would probably crash or best give incorrect results. But, you might say, why would someone do this? They know that they should enter a number, so why would they enter a letter? The answer, is that they would, they'd want to see what would happen. Users do this sort of thing all the time.

In addition to trying to anticipate what things people might do, clearly and very importantly, you'd need to check that the program gave correct results when you gave it normal data.

Good programmers follow a systematic procedure to try to test their programs thoroughly. The table below shows how we might test our quadratic program in a systematic way.

Values	Reason for Test	Program Output	Result
1 3 2	Integer values - integer result	Roots : -1.00 and -2.00	Pass
1 4 1	Integer values - real result	Roots : -0.27 and -3.73	Pass
1 4 4	Integer values - one double root	Roots : -2.00 and -2.00	Pass
1 1 1	integer values - no roots	No roots	Pass
0 1 1	Integer values - divide by zero	Runtime error	Fail
-1 -3 4	Negative integer values	Roots : -4.00 and 1.00	Pass
1.2 3.1 -5.1	Real values - real roots	Roots : 1.14 and -3.72	Pass
a 1 2	Non-integer values	Runtime error	Fail

Clearly the program failed when given a zero value for a and when we gave it non-integer values. If we were writing a commercial program we'd have to anticipate user input along these lines and re-write our code to compensate. We could for instance tell the user that she's trying to divide by zero and would she please try again and in the case of invalid input, we'd suggest that she sticks to real numbers.

If you were writing a program that calculated the grade average of a number of students, you might systematically check that the numbers such as 0% or 100% did not cause problems. These would be **extreme** values. You would check for normal numbers, negative numbers and invalid input such as letters. You might also check that your program handled real numbers correctly, both when input and when output.

Before any program is made generally available it must be fully tested to the very best of your ability. What tests you run are usually up to you, but they need to be as comprehensive as possible. It is impossible to identify everything that the user might do, but you need to try.

A gym has many different types of exercise equipment. To use any equipment, members need to enter an individual 4-digit number. A computer system records how long each member has spent on each type of equipment and uses this information to charge the members.

Complete the table below with input values which could be used to test that the computer system correctly checks that the member has entered their number correctly. For each item of test data

- **Explain why it is used**
- **State the expected outcome** [A451 Specimen Paper 2010 Q9 (6)]

Test data	Reason for test	Expected outcome

Possible test cases might include the following.

Test data	Reason for test	Expected outcome
Exactly 4 digits (and in the member file)	To confirm that it works	Success
298	To see if numbers shorter than 4 digits are rejected	Error message: The number entered is too short.
More than 4 digits	To see if numbers longer than 4 digits are rejected	Error message: The number entered is too long.
Input missing	To see if input is required	Error message: No number has been entered
Non numeric characters	To see if non numeric characters are accepted	Error message: The data contains non numerical characters
A PIN which does not exist in the customer file	To see if any 4 digit number can be entered	Error message: The number entered does not exist in the customer file

8

General questions

It is possible that you may be asked a general question that doesn't fall within any particular part of the specification. The examiners expect that at the end of the course you will have developed a good understanding of technology and how it has changed our lives sometimes for the better but occasionally to the detriment of ourselves or society. The following question is one that was asked in January 2011 and needed a carefully worded, intelligent answer to be awarded full marks.

A school uses a computer system to monitor the attendance, punctuality and homework of its pupils. Describe two ways in which modern computer technology can help the school monitor the pupils. [A451 Jan 2012 Q7 (4)]

As with all of these types of questions there is no set answer and the following are just examples. The examiners gave up to 2 marks per technology, either 1 mark for naming the technology and 1 mark for explaining it or 2 marks for explaining in detail without naming the technology.

- Swipe card / Smart card technology / RFID cards
- ... can allow pupils to register themselves
- ... and can also allow pupils to be located
- Electronic registers and a centralised attendance database
- ... can be immediately updated
- ... messages (e.g. via email / SMS to parents) can be sent to inform of absence
- ... can produce up to date reports of absence
- A virtual learning environment can be used
- ... and homework can be recorded online
- ... whether homework is completed is recorded on line
- ... and parents can be given access to this information

Computer technology has changed the ways in which teenagers
interact with each other. Explain how developments in software
and hardware have enabled new methods of communication among
teenagers. The quality of written communication will be assessed
in your answer to this question. [A451 Jan 2011 Q9 (6)]

The examiners expected the following points to be made.

- Hardware: Computers faster and more capable of high speed Internet
  access – allows video and voice communication; large server farms and
  cheaper storage enables the infrastructure behind large social networking websites; convergence of computers with other digital technology
  (e.g. phones, television sets) allows continuity of networking over several formats.
- Software: Open standards and increased use of server side software
  (e.g. php) allow social networking sites to operate across all platforms.
  Open protocols allow several clients to use the same services or allow
  software to be written to allow different services to sync with each
  other; coexist. Software increasingly easier to use and easily adopted
  by younger generation.

Index